Mothers Please!

Mothers Please!

One Hundred Poems for Every Mother

Edited by
Douglas Brooks-Davies

Illustrated by
Katarzyna Klein

ORION

AN ORION PAPERBACK

First published in Great Britain in 2002 by Orion,
an imprint of Orion Books Ltd, Orion House,
5 Upper St Martin's Lane, London WC2H 9EA

A CIP catalogue record for this book
is available from the British Library.

ISBN 0 75284 888 7

Printed in Italy by Printer Trento srl

Publisher's Note: A substantial amount of the material in this
book has already appeared under the title *Talking of Mothers.*

～ Contents

Introduction

⁓ *Introduction*

As the old saying goes, everybody (apart from Adam) has, or has had, a mother, and the one hundred poems in this anthology celebrate the range of emotions motherhood calls forth in us from love to guilt to anger to laughter, and many more.

From the point of view of Western European poetry, mothers emerge out of myth: Eve, Ceres (known as Demeter to the Greeks), Niobe, and (the point where myth becomes history) the Virgin Mary, and some poems in this anthology are explicitly about these mothers. Equally mythical though, are the origins of our festival of motherhood, Mothering Sunday, the first mention of which, according to the *Oxford English Dictionary*, is in Robert Herrick's little poem 'To Dianeme. A Ceremony in Gloucester' (first published in 1648 and printed here). Herrick alludes in addition to Mothering Sunday's customary gift, the rich fruit cake known as simnel.

However, the brevity of Herrick's poem yields no obvious clue to the long and ancient tradition that underpins it. For, as the antiquarian William Hone explained in his *The Every-Day Book; or, Everlasting Calendar of Popular Amusements* (1826) under the heading Mid-Lent Sunday or Mothering Sunday:

> It is still a custom on Mid-Lent Sunday in many parts of England, for servants and apprentices to carry cakes or some nice eatables or trinkets, as presents to their parents; and in other parts, to visit their mother for a meal of furmity [frumenty, or wheat cooked in milk and seasoned with cinnamon and sugar], or to receive cakes from her with a blessing. This is called going a-mothering.

Hone goes on to explain that 'going a-mothering is from the Roman Catholic custom of going to the mother-church on Mid-Lent Sunday, to make offerings at the high altar', and he adds: 'and that custom of the Romish Church is derived from the Hilaria'.

The Hilaria celebrated Cybele, the earth mother and reputed mother of the gods, on 25 March annually; so that at the root of more modern feasts of mothering (and the feast of the Annunciation to the Virgin Mary on Lady Day, also 25 March) lies a myth of our origins with mother earth and, as Hone reminds us, the image of mother church, as in Galatians 4, and I Peter 2:2, with its reference to the maternal milk of the divine word.

The appropriation of pagan practice by Christianity – as in the case of mother earth becoming mother church – is a common one; so, too, the slippage from mother church to ordinary child-bearing woman is an instance of the familiar process by which things once the province of the divine become secularised. Thomas Hardy comments on it in *Tess of the D'Urbervilles* (1891), when he observes that the May walk of local women is a solitary remnant of an ancient, now unrecognised, Cerealia (chapter 2).

Such slippage means that few of us recognise, as we give our flowers and floral cards on Mother's Day, of the link between our own maternal spring festival and the ancient perception of seed-nourishing and flower-producing mother earth, who in one form was indeed the Cybele of the Hilaria, but in another was Ceres, the goddess of flowers and grain (cereals). She was Cybele's daughter, and her Greek name, Demeter, was long misunderstood as meaning earth-mother. Ceres-Demeter's own daughter (Proserpina in Latin, Persephone in Greek) was abducted by the god of the underworld while gathering flowers. According to the myth, after much searching and heartache on Ceres' part, she was restored to her grieving mother for half the year, during which time vegetation flourishes. When she returns to the underworld, Ceres' grieving begins again, and the earth is covered in winter gloom and desolation. It is no accident, then, that a meal of wheat-based frumenty, that dish of Ceres, was traditional on Mothering Sunday, according to Hone and others.

Ceres-Demeter appears here in an extract from Tennyson's *Demeter and Persephone* (1889); for Tennyson, that supreme poet of melancholy and bereavement, evokes the level of grieving maternal desolation almost better than anyone. His poem balances the extract from Arthur Golding's translation of the Roman poet Ovid's *Metamorphoses* concerning Niobe, punished for her pride in her children by being transformed into permanently weeping stone. Published three centuries earlier than Tennyson's version of an equally old story, Golding's allegory of the sheer numbness of maternal heartbreak complements Demeter's sense of loss while withholding any hope of the return of even one of her offspring.

It may be thought perverse to start an introduction to an anthology of poems on mothers and motherhood with evocations of such gloom. Yet a reading of many of the poems will be enough to show how far our sentimental image of motherhood is from the experience of earlier centuries. Some women bear children easily. Others, because of physical or financial circumstances, still don't. These latter will recognise the emotions registered in many of the poems printed here: fear of childbirth, fear of perinatal mortality (both infant and maternal). After all, forget the privileges of modern medicine, and we are back with the world that begot the tale of Niobe – a world where the gods are cruel and punish you by stealing the lives of your young ones, and in which no vegetation myth offers the comfort of cyclical restoration.

There are, of course, exceptions: Mary Barber's fond piece on her son first putting on breeches, Ambrose Philips's poem 'To Miss Charlotte Pulteney in Her Mother's Arms, 1 May 1724' (where the precision of the dating gives it the precious particularity of a photograph), Mrs Barbauld on 'Washing Day', and, perhaps best of all, Ann Yearsley siding with mothers against nurses on the bringing up of children.

How perennial that battle is! We find it again – to cite only poems reprinted in this anthology – in Locker-Lampson's wicked little piece 'A Terrible Infant', Elizabeth Barrett Browning's 'Isobel's Child,' where mother takes over the night care while the nurse sleeps, the poems Robert Louis Stevenson attached to his *Child's Garden of Verses*, and Edith Nesbit's well-known 'Song', with its moment of private maternal tenderness stolen from the world of the nanny and the nursery. These poems are, in their various ways, as refreshing as Francis Quarles's 'On the Infancy of Our Saviour' with its sudden glimpses of real family life as it imagines the baby 'perking' on Mary's knee, nuzzling her breast, and, as his legs gain strength, sees him 'diddl[ing] up and down the room'.

So many of these poems register tenderness, and so many of them pain. Illegitimacy was a major social problem until very recently; child death was inescapable; hard labour was the reality of life for the majority of women. As we read on in this anthology, we hear women speaking increasingly for themselves – about unmarried mothers being driven to murder (Helen Leigh); about the anguish of having to earn a living knowing that your illegitimate daughter is being brought up elsewhere (Ellen Johnston); about the difficulty of summoning up maternal feelings (Alice Meynell, 'The Modern Mother'); about the loss of the maiden (maternal) name (Jane Cave).

Counterbalancing these, however, we have the robust humour of Judy Rose's 'Mummy Said The "B" Word', Liz

Lochhead's telling 'Everybody's Mother' (which, in a sense, says it all), Elizabeth Jennings' 'Clothes' (itself counterpointing her poignant 'To My Mother at 73' with its combination of mutual need and love, the fear of hurting, the resentment at not being allowed to grow up, and the guilt consequent upon that resentment), Grace Nichols' sharp yet tender 'Granny Please Comb My Hair'.

The trouble with naming individual poems is that, in the end, one wants to celebrate all of them, for they are all, in their different ways, touching, poignant, funny, *good*. So I shall simply conclude with a favourite that most children (and many parents) will recognise, Brian Patten's 'Squeezes':

> We love to squeeze bananas,
> We love to squeeze ripe plums,
> And when they are feeling sad
> We love to squeeze our mums.

DOUGLAS BROOKS-DAVIES

Mothers Please!

'Noel, el, el, el, el, el, el . . .'

Noel, el, el, el, el, el, el, el, el, el, el, el,
Mary was greet with Gabriel.

Mary mother, meek and mild,
From shame and sin that ye us shield,
For great on ground ye gone with child,
  Gabriel nuntio.

Mary mother, be not adread:
Jesu is in your body bred,
And of your breast he will be fed
  Cum pudoris lilio.

Mary mother, the fruit of thee
For us was nailed on a tree;
In heaven is now His majesty:
  Fulget resurrectio.

Mary mother, the third day
Up He rose, as I you say;
To hell he took the right way,
  Motu fertur proprio.

Mary mother, after thine Son
Up thou styest with Him to wone;
The angels were glad when thou were come
  In coeli palatio.

'Flower of Roses, Angels' Joy'

Flower of roses, angels' joy,
Tower of David, ark of Noy;
　First of saints, whose true protecting
Of the young and weak in sprite
Makes my soul these lines indite
　To Thy throne her plaint directing.

Orphan child alone I lie,
Childlike to thee I cry,
　Queen of heaven, used to cherish;
Eyes of grace, behold, I fall;
Ears of pity, hear my call
　Lest in swaddling clouts I perish.

Hide the greatness of each fault;
My desert, if there be aught,
　By thy merits be enlarged
That the debts wherein I fall,
Paying nought but owing all,
　By thy prayer be discharged.

Pray to Him whose shape I bear,
By thy love, thy care, thy fear,
　By thy glorious birth and breeding,
That though our sins touch the sky
Yet His mercies mount more high,
　All His other works exceeding.

Tell Him that, in strengthening me
With His grace, He graceth thee,
    Every little one defending;
Tell Him that I cloy thine ears
With the cry of childish tears
    From His footstool still ascending.

Hear my cries and grant me aid,
Perfect mother, perfect maid;
    Hear my cries to thee addressed;
From my plaints turn not thy face,
Humble and yet full of grace,
    Pure, untouched, for ever blessed.

On My Own Little Daughter, Four Years Old

Sweet lovely infant, innocently gay,
  With blooming face arrayed in peaceful smiles,
How light thy cheerful heart doth sportive play,
  Unconscious of all future cares and toils.

With what delight I've seen thy little feet
  Dancing with pleasure at my near approach!
Eager they ran my well-known form to meet,
  Secure of welcome, fearless of reproach.

Then happy hast thou prattled in mine ear
  Thy little anxious tales of pain or joy;
Thy fears lest faithful Tray thy frock should tear,
  Thy pride when ladies give the gilded toy.

How oft, when sad reflection dimmed mine eye,
  As memory recalled past scenes of woe,
Thy tender heart hath heaved the expressive sigh
  Of sympathy, for ills thou could'st not know.

Oft too in silence I've admired that face,
  Beaming with pity for a mother's grief,
Whilst in each anxious feature I could trace
  Compassion eager to afford relief.

E'en now methinks I hear the artless tongue,
  Lisping sweet sounds of comfort to mine ear:
'Oh, fret no more – your Fanny is not gone –
  She will not go – don't cry – your Fanny's here.'

If, ere her mind attains its full-grown strength,
    Thy will consigns me to an early tomb,
If in Thy sight my thread's near run its length
    And called by Thee I cannot watch her bloom —

O heavenly Father, guard my infant child;
    Protect her steps through this wide scene of care;
Within her breast implant each virtue mild,
    And teach her all she ought to hope or fear.

'My Mother Said'

My mother said I never should
Play with the gypsies in the wood;
If I did, then she would say,
'Naughty girl to disobey.
Your hair shan't curl
And your shoes shan't shine,
You gypsy girl,
You shan't be mine.'
And my father said that if I did
He'd rap my head with the tea-pot lid.

My mother said I never should
Play with the gypsies in the wood.
The wood was dark, the grass was green,
In came Sally with a tambourine.
I went to the sea – no ship to get across;
I paid ten shillings for a blind white horse;
I up on his back and was off in a crack –
Sally tell my mother I shall never come back.

'There Was a Little Girl'

There was a little girl, and she had a little curl
Right in the middle of her forehead;
When she was good she was very, very good,
And when she was bad she was horrid.

She stood on her head, on her little truckle-bed,
With nobody by for to hinder.
She screamed and she squalled, she yelled and she bawled,
And drummed her little heels against the winder.

Her mother heard the noise and thought it was the boys,
A-kicking up a rumpus in the attic;
But when she climbed the stair, and saw Jemima there,
She took her and did whip her most emphatic.

'My Mother Sent Me For Some Water'

My mother sent me for some water,
For some water from the sea;
My foot slipped, and in I tumbled;
Three jolly sailors came to me.
One said he'd buy me silks and satins,
One said he'd buy me a guinea gold ring,
One said he'd buy me a silver cradle
For to rock my baby in.

The Cruel Mother

There was a lady lived in York
  All alone and a loney,
A farmer's son he courted her,
  All down by the greenwood sidey.

He courted her for seven long years,
At last she proved with child by him.

She pitched her knee against a tree,
And there she found great misery.

She pitched her back against a thorn,
And there she had her baby born.

She drew the fillet off her head,
And bound the baby's hands and legs.

She drew a knife both long and sharp,
She pierced the baby's innocent heart.

She wiped the knife upon the grass,
The more she wiped the blood run fast.

She washed her hands all in the spring,
Thinking to turn a maid again.

As she was going to her father's hall,
She saw three babes a-playing at ball.

One dressed in silk, the other in satin,
The other stark-naked as ever was born.

'O dear baby, if you was mine,
I'd dress you in silk and satins so fine.'

'O dear mother, I once was thine,
You never would dress me, coarse or fine.

'The coldest earth it was my bed,
The green grass was my coverlet.

'O mother, mother, for your sin,
Heaven gate you shall not enter in.

'There is a fire beyond hell's gate,
And there you'll burn both early and late.'

The Death of Queen Jane

Queen Jane lay in labour full nine days or more,
Till the women were so tired, they could stay no longer there.

'Good women, good women, good women as ye be,
Do open my right side, and find my baby.'

'Oh no,' said the women, 'that never may be,
We will send for King Henry and hear what he say.'

King Henry was sent for, King Henry did come:
'What do ail you, my lady, your eyes look so dim?'

'King Henry, King Henry, will you do one thing for me?
That's to open my right side, and find my baby.'

'Oh no,' said King Henry, 'that's a thing I'll never do.
If I lose the flower of England, I shall lose the branch too.'

King Henry went mourning, and so did his men,
And so did the dear baby, for Queen Jane did die then.

And how deep was the mourning, how black were the bands,
How yellow, yellow were the flamboys they carried in their
    hands.

There was fiddling, aye, and dancing on the day the babe was
    born,
But poor Queen Jane beloved lay as cold as a stone.

'Mummy, Oh Mummy'

'Mummy, Oh Mummy, what's this pollution
That everyone's talking about?'
'Pollution's the mess that the country is in,
That we'd all be far better without.
It's factories belching their fumes in the air,
And the beaches all covered with tar,
Now throw all those sweet papers into the bushes
Before we get back in the car.'

'Mummy, Oh Mummy, who makes pollution,
And why don't they stop if it's bad?'
''Cos people like that just don't think about others,
They just don't think at all, I might add.
They spray all the crops and they poison the flowers,
And wipe out the birds and the bees,
Now there's a good place we could dump that old mattress
Right out of sight in the trees.'

'Mummy, Oh Mummy, what's going to happen
If all the pollution goes on?'
'Well the world will end up like a second-hand junk-yard,
With all of its treasures quite gone.
The fields will be littered with plastic and tins,
The streams will be covered with foam,
Now throw those two pop bottles over the hedge,
Save us from carting them home.'

'But Mummy, Oh Mummy, if I throw the bottles,
Won't that be polluting the wood?'
'Nonsense! that isn't the same thing at all,
You just shut up and be good.
If you're going to start getting silly ideas
I'm taking you home right away,
'Cos pollution is something that other folk do,
We're just enjoying our day.'

Whistle, Daughter, Whistle

'O mother, I longs to get married,
I longs to be a bride.
I longs to lay with that young man
And close to by his side,
Oh happy should I be,
For I'm young and merry and almost weary
Of my virginity.'

'O daughter, I was twenty
Before that I was wed
And many a long and lonesome mile
I carried my maidenhead.'
'O mother, that may be,
It's not the case by me,
For I'm young and merry and almost weary
Of my virginity.'

'Daughter, daughter, whistle,
And you shall have a sheep.'
'I cannot whistle, mother,
But I can sadly weep.
My maidenhead does grieve me,
That fills my heart with fear.
It is a burden, a heavy burden,
It's more than I can bear.'

'Daughter, daughter, whistle,
And you shall have a cow.'
'I cannot whistle, mother,
For 'deed I don't know how.
My maidenhead does grieve me,

That fills my heart with fear.
It is a burden, a heavy burden,
It's more than I can bear.'

'Daughter, daughter, whistle,
And you shall have a man.'
             (*whistles*)
'You see very well I can.'
'You nasty, impudent Jane,
I'll pull your courage down.
Take off your silks and satins,
Put on your working gown.
I'll send you to the fields,
A-tossing of the hay
With your fork and rake the hay to make
And then hear what you say.'

'Mother, don't be so cruel
To send me to the fields
Where young men may entice me
And to them I may yield.
For mother, it's quite well known
I am not too young grown,
For it is a pity a maid so pretty
As I should lay alone.'

Ask Mummy Ask Daddy

When I ask Daddy
Daddy says ask Mummy.

When I ask Mummy
Mummy says ask Daddy
I don't know where to go.

Better ask my teddy
he never says no.

Emma Hackett's Newsbook

Last night my mum
Got really mad
And threw a jam tart
At my Dad.
Dad lost his temper
Then with mother,
Threw one at her
And hit my brother.
My brother thought
It was my sister,
Threw two at her
But somehow missed her.
My sister,
She is only three,
Hurled four at him
And one at me!

Our Mother

Our mother is a detective.
She is a great finder of clues.
She found the mud and grass on our shoes,
When we were told not to go in the park –
Because it would be getting dark –
But come straight home.

She found the jam on our thumbs,
And in our beds the tiniest crumbs
From the cakes we said we had not eaten.
When we blamed the cat for breaking the fruit bowl –
Because we did not want any fuss –
She *knew* it was us.

'The Mother of Mary'

The mother of Mary, that merciful may,
  Pray for us both night and day.

Sweet Saint Anne, we thee beseech
  Thou pray for us to Our Lady
That she will be our soulès leech
  That day when we shall die;
      Herefore we say:

Through thee was gladded all this world
  When Mary of thee bornè was,
That bore that bairn, that blissful Lord
  That grants us all mercy and grace;
      Herefore we say:

Barren thou wert full long before;
  Then God He say to thy meekness
That thou shouldest deliver that was forlore:
  Man's soul, that lay in fiendish distress;
      Herefore we say:

Fore Joachim, that holy husband,
  Prayed to God full patiently
That He would send his sweet son,
  Some fruit between you two to be;
      Herefore we say:

Then God He granted graciously
  Between you two a flower should spring;
The root thereof is cleped Jesse,
  That joy and bliss to the world shall bring;
      Herefore I say:

The blissful branch this flower on grew
  Out of Jesse, at my weeting,
Was Mary mild, that bare Jesu,
  Maiden and mother to heaven King;
    Herefore I say:

Ycalled Jesu of Nazareth,
  God's Son of high degree,
As here as man that suffered death
  And reigned into David dignity;
    Herefore I say:

In Bethlem, in that blessed place,
  Mary mild this flower hath born,
Between an ox and an ass,
  To save his people that was forlorn;
    Herefore I say:

Mater, ora Filium,
  That He will after this outlere
Nobis donet gaudium
  Sine fine for His mercy.
    Herefore I say:
  The mother of Mary, that merciful may,
  Pray for us both night and day.

from *A Winter's Day*

The family cares call next upon the wife
To quit her mean but comfortable bed.
And first she stirs the fire and blows the flame,
Then from her heap of sticks, for winter stored,
An armful brings; loud-crackling as they burn,
Thick fly the red sparks upward to the roof,
While slowly mounts the smoke in wreathy clouds.
On goes the seething pot with morning cheer,
For which some little wishful hearts await,
Who, peeping from the bedclothes, spy well-pleased
The cheery light that blazes on the wall,
And bawl for leave to rise. —
Their busy mother knows not where to turn,
Her morning work comes now so thick upon her.
One she must help to tie his little coat,
Unpin his cap, and seek another's shoe.
When all is o'er, out to the door they run,
With new-combed sleeky hair and glistening cheeks,
Each with some little project in his head . . .

A Mother to Her Waking Infant

Now in thy dazzling half-oped eye,
Thy curled nose and lip awry,
Thy up-hoist arm and nodding head,
And little chin with crystal spread,
Poor helpless thing! what do I see,
    That I should sing of thee?

From thy poor tongue no accents come,
Which can but rub thy toothless gum;
Small understanding boasts thy face,
Thy shapeless limbs nor step nor grace;
A few short words thy feats may tell,
    And yet I love thee well.

When sudden wakes the bitter shriek,
And redder swells thy little cheek;
When rattled keys thy woes beguile,
And through the wet eye gleams the smile,
Still for thy weakly self is spent
    Thy silly little plaint.

But when thy friends are in distress,
Thou'lt laugh and chuckle ne'er the less,
Nor e'en with sympathy be smitten,
Though all are sad but thee and kitten.
Yet, little varlet that thou art,
    Thou twitchest at the heart.

Thy rosy cheeks so soft and warm;
Thy pinky hand and dimpled arm;
Thy silken locks that scantly peep,

With gold-tipped ends, where circles deep
Around thy neck in harmless grace
So soft and sleekly hold their place,
Might harder hearts with kindness fill,
    And gain our right good will.

Each passing clown bestows his blessing,
Thy mouth is worn with old wives' kissing:
E'en lighter looks the gloomy eye
Of surly sense, when thou art by;
And yet I think whoe'er they be,
    They love thee not like me.

Perhaps when time shall add a few
Short years to thee, thou'lt love me too.
Then wilt thou through life's weary way
Become my sure and cheering stay:
Wilt care for me, and be my hold,
    When I am weak and old.

Thou'lt listen to my lengthened tale,
And pity me when I am frail –
But see, the sweepy spinning fly
Upon the window takes thine eye.
Go to thy little senseless play –
    Thou dost not heed my lay.

from *Washing Day*

                              Woe to the friend
Whose evil stars have urged him forth to claim
On such a day the hospitable rites!
Looks, blank at best, and stinted courtesy,
Shall he receive. Vainly he feeds his hopes
With dinner of roast chicken, savoury pie,
Or tart or pudding: pudding he nor tart
That day shall eat; nor, though the husband try,
Mending what can't be helped, to kindle mirth
From cheer deficient, shall his consort's brow
Clear up propitious: the unlucky guest
In silence dines, and early slinks away.
I well remember, when a child, the awe
This day struck into me; for then the maids,
I scarce knew why, looked cross, and drove me from them;
Nor soft caress could I obtain, nor hope
Usual indulgences: jelly or creams,
Relic of costly suppers, and set by
For me, their petted one; or buttered toast,
When butter was forbid; or thrilling tale
Of ghost, or witch, or murder. So I went
And sheltered me beside the parlour fire:
There my dear grandmother, eldest of forms,
Tended the little ones, and watched from harm,
Anxiously fond, though oft her spectacles
With elfin cunning hid, and oft the pins
Drawn from her ravelled stocking, might have soured
One less indulgent. –
At intervals my mother's voice was heard,
Urging dispatch. Briskly the work went on,

All hands employed to wash, to rinse, to wring,
To fold, and starch, and clap, and iron, and plait.
Then would I sit me down, and ponder much
Why washings were. Sometimes through hollow bowl
Of pipe amused we blew, and sent aloft
The floating bubbles, little dreaming then
To see, Montgolfier, thy silken ball
Ride buoyant through the clouds – so near approach
The sports of children and the toils of men.
Earth, air, and sky, and ocean, hath its bubbles,
And verse is one of them – this most of all.

To a Little Invisible Being Who is Expected Soon to Become Visible

Germ of new life, whose powers expanding slow
For many a moon their full perfection wait –
Haste, precious pledge of happy love, to go
Auspicious borne through life's mysterious gate.

What powers lie folded in thy curious frame –
Senses from objects locked, and mind from thought!
How little canst thou guess thy lofty claim
To grasp at all the worlds the Almighty wrought!

And see, the genial season's warmth to share,
Fresh younglings shoot, and opening roses glow!
Swarms of new life exulting fill the air –
Haste, infant bud of being, haste to blow!

For thee the nurse prepares her lulling songs,
The eager matrons count the lingering day;
But far the most thy anxious parent longs
On thy soft cheek a mother's kiss to lay.

She only asks to lay her burden down,
That her glad arms that burden may resume;
And nature's sharpest pangs her wishes crown,
That free thee living from thy living tomb.

She longs to fold to her maternal breast
Part of herself, yet to herself unknown;
To see and to salute the stranger guest,
Fed with her life through many a tedious moon.

Come, reap thy rich inheritance of love!
Bask in the fondness of a mother's eye!
Nor wit nor eloquence her heart shall move
Like the first accents of thy feeble cry.

Haste, little captive, burst thy prison doors!
Launch on the living world, and spring to light!
Nature for thee displays her various stores,
Opens her thousand inlets of delight.

If charmed verse or muttered prayers had power
With favouring spells to speed thee on thy way,
Anxious I'd bid my beads each passing hour,
Till thy wished smile thy mother's pangs o'erpay.

Written for My Son, and Spoken by Him at His First Putting on Breeches

What is it our mammas bewitches,
To plague us little boys with breeches?
To tyrant custom we must yield
Whilst vanquished Reason flies the field.
Our legs must suffer by ligation,
To keep the blood from circulation;
And then our feet, though young and tender,
We to the shoemaker surrender,
Who often makes our shoes so strait
Our growing feet they cramp and fret;
Whilst, with contrivance most profound,
Across our insteps we are bound,
Which is the cause, I make no doubt,
Why thousands suffer in the gout.
Our wiser ancestors wore brogues,
Before the surgeons bribed these rogues
With narrow toes and heels like pegs
To help to make us break our legs.

Then, ere we know how to use our fists,
Our mothers closely bind our wrists,
And never think our clothes are neat
Till they're so tight we cannot eat.
And, to increase our other pains,
The hat-band helps to cramp our brains.
The cravat finishes the work,
Like bowstring sent from the Grand Turk.

Thus dress, that should prolong our date,
Is made to hasten on our fate.
Fair privilege of nobler natures,
To be more plagued than other creatures!
The wild inhabitants of air
Are clothed by heaven with wondrous care:
The beauteous, well-compacted feathers
Are coats of mail against all weathers;
Enamelled, to delight the eye,
Gay as the bow that decks the sky.
The beasts are clothed with beauteous skins;
The fishes armed with scales and fins,
Whose lustre lends the sailor light
When all the stars are hid in night.

Oh, were our dress contrived like these,
For use, for ornament, and ease!
Man only seems to sorrow born,
Naked, defenceless, and forlorn.

Yet we have Reason to supply
What nature did to man deny:
Weak viceroy! Who thy power will own
When Custom has usurped thy throne?
In vain did I appeal to thee
Ere I would wear his livery;
Who, in defiance of thy rules,
Delights to make us act like fools.
O'er human race the tyrant reigns,
And binds them in eternal chains.
We yield to his despotic sway,
The only monarch all obey.

To My Mother

Most near, most dear, most loved and most far,
Under the window where I often found her
Sitting as huge as Asia, seismic with laughter,
Gin and chicken helpless in her Irish hand,
Irresistible as Rabelais, but most tender for
The lame dogs and hurt birds that surround her, –
She is a procession no one can follow after
But be like a little dog following a brass band.

She will not glance up at the bomber, or condescend
To drop her gin and scuttle to a cellar,
But lean on the mahogany table like a mountain
Whom only faith can move, and so I send
O all my faith and all my love to tell her
That she will move from mourning into morning.

The Mother's Dream

I'd a dream tonight
  As I vell asleep –
Oh! the touchen zight
  Still do mëake me weep, –
Ov my little bwoy
That's a-took awoy;
Aye, about my joy
  I wer not to keep.

As in heaven high
  I my child did seek,
There, in traïn, come by
  Childern feäir an' meek;
Each in lilywhite,
Wi' a lamp alight;
Each wer clear to zight,
  But noo words did speak.

Then a-looken sad
  Come my child in turn;
But the lamp he had,
  Oh! he didden burn;
He, to clear my doubt,
Zaid, a-turn'd about,
Your tears put en out;
  Mother, never murn.

False Security

I remember the dread with which I at a quarter past four
Let go with a bang behind me our house front door
And, clutching a present for my dear little hostess tight,
Sailed out for the children's party into the night
Or rather the gathering night. For still some boys
In the near municipal acres were making a noise

Shuffling in fallen leaves and shouting and whistling
And running past hedges of hawthorn, spikey and bristling.

And black in the oncoming darkness stood out the trees
And pink shone the ponds in the sunset ready to freeze
And all was still and ominous waiting for dark
And the keeper was ringing his closing bell in the park
And the arc lights started to fizzle and burst into mauve
As I climbed West Hill to the great big house on The Grove,
Where the children's party was and the dear little hostess.
But halfway up stood the empty house where the ghost is
I crossed to the other side and under the arc
Made a rush for the next kind lamp-post out of the dark
And so to the next and the next till I reached the top
Where The Grove branched off to the left. Then ready to
 drop
I ran to the ironwork gateway of number seven
Secure at last on the lamplit fringe of Heaven.

Oh who can say how subtle and safe one feels
Shod in one's children's sandals from Daniel Neal's,
Clad in one's party clothes made of stuff from Heal's?
And who can still one's thrill at the candle shine
On cakes and ices and jelly and blackcurrant wine,
And the warm little feel of my hostess's hand in mine?
Can I forget my delight in the conjuring show?
And wasn't I proud that I was the last to go?
Too over-excited and pleased with myself to know
That the words I heard my hostess's mother employ
To a guest departing, would ever diminish my joy,
I WONDER WHERE JULIA FOUND THAT STRANGE, RATHER
COMMON LITTLE BOY?

Percival Mandeville, the Perfect Boy

Percival Mandeville, the perfect boy,
Was all a schoolmaster could wish to see –
Upright and honourable, good at games,
Well-built, blue-eyed; a sense of leadership
Lifted him head and shoulders from the crowd.
His work was good. His written answers, made
In a round, tidy and decided hand,
Pleased the examiners. His open smile
Enchanted others. He could also frown
On anything unsporting, mean or base,
Unworthy of the spirit of the school
And what it stood for. Oh the dreadful hour
When once upon a time he frowned on me!

Just what had happened I cannot recall –
Maybe some bullying in the dormitory;
But well I recollect his warning words:
'I'll fight you, Betjeman, you swine, for that,
Behind the bike sheds before morning school.'
So all the previous night I spewed with fear.
I could not box: I greatly dreaded pain.
A recollection of the winding punch
Jack Drayton once delivered, blows and boots
Upon the bum at Highgate Junior School,
All multiplied by x from Mandeville,
Emptied my bladder. Silent in the dorm
I cleaned my teeth and clambered into bed.
Thin seemed pyjamas and inadequate
The regulation blankets once so warm,
'What's up?' 'Oh, nothing.' I expect they knew…

And, in the morning, cornflakes, bread and tea,
Cook's Farm Eggs and a spoon of marmalade,
Which heralded the North and Hilliard hours
Of Latin composition, brought the post.
Breakfast and letters! Then it was a flash
Of hope, escape and inspiration came:
Invent a letter of bad news from home.
I hung my head and tried to look as though,
By keeping such a brave stiff upper lip
And just not blubbing, I was noble too.
I sought out Mandeville. 'I say,' I said,
'I'm frightfully sorry I can't fight today.
I've just received some rotten news from home:
My mater's very ill.' No need for more –
His arm was round my shoulder comforting:
'All right, old chap. Of course I understand.'

The Little Boy Found

The little boy lost in the lonely fen,
Led by the wandering light,
Began to cry; but God, ever nigh,
Appeared like his father in white.

He kissed the child, and by the hand led,
And to his mother brought,
Who in sorrow pale, through the lonely dale,
Her little boy weeping sought.

Infant Sorrow

My mother groaned, my father wept,
Into the dangerous world I leaped:
Helpless, naked, piping loud,
Like a fiend hid in a cloud.

Struggling in my father's hands,
Striving against my swaddling bands,
Bound and weary I thought best
To sulk upon my mother's breast.

The Land of Dreams

'Awake, awake, my little boy,
Thou wast thy mother's only joy;
Why dost thou weep in thy gentle sleep?
Awake! thy father does thee keep.'

'Oh, what land is the land of dreams?
What are its mountains and what are its streams?
Oh, father, I saw my mother there,
Among the lilies by waters fair.

'Among the lambs, clothed in white,
She walked with her Thomas in sweet delight.
I wept for joy, like a dove I mourn;
Oh, when shall I again return?'

'Dear child, I also by pleasant streams
Have wandered all night in the land of dreams;
But though calm and warm the waters wide,
I could not get to the other side.'

'Father, O father, what do we here
In this land of unbelief and fear?
The land of dreams is better far,
Above the light of the morning star.'

from *The Four Ages of Man (Childhood)*

Ah me! conceived in sin, and born in sorrow:
A nothing; here today but gone tomorrow.
Whose mean beginning blushing can't reveal,
But night and darkness must with shame conceal.
My mother's breeding sickness I will spare;
Her nine months' weary burden not declare.
To show her bearing pangs I should do wrong,
To tell that pain which can't be told by tongue.
With tears into this world I did arrive;
My mother still did waste, as I did thrive:
Who yet with love, and all alacrity,
Spending was willing to be spent for me:
With wayward cries I did disturb her rest,
Who sought still to appease me with her breast:
With weary arms she danced, and 'bye, bye' sung
When wretched I (ungrate) had done the wrong . . .

Before the Birth of One of Her Children

All things within this fading world hath end,
Adversity doth still our joys attend;
No ties so strong, no friends so clear and sweet,
But with death's parting blow is sure to meet.
The sentence past is most irrevocable,
A common thing yet, oh, inevitable;
How soon, my dear, death may my steps attend,
How soon it may be thy lot to lose thy friend,
We both are ignorant; yet love bids me
These farewell lines to recommend to thee,
That when that knot's untied that made us one,
I may seem thine, who in effect am none.
And if I see not half my days that's due,
What nature would, God grant to yours and you;
The many faults that well you know I have,
Let be interred in my oblivious grave;
If any worth or virtue were in me,
Let that live freshly in thy memory
And when thou feelest no grief, as I no harms,
Yet love thy dead, who long lay in thine arms:
And when thy loss shall be repaid with gains,
Look to my little babes, my dear remains.
And if thou love thyself, or loved'st me,
These O protect from stepdame's injury.
And if Chance to thine eyes shall bring this verse,
With some sad sighs honour my absent hearse;
And kiss this paper for thy love's dear sake,
Who with salt tears this last farewell did take.

A Sweet Lullaby

Come, little babe, come, silly soul,
Thy father's shame, thy mother's grief,
Born, as I doubt, to all our dole,
And to thyself unhappy chief;
  Sing lullaby and lap it warm,
  Poor soul that thinks no creature harm.

Thou little think'st and less dost know
The cause of this thy mother's moan;
Thou want'st the wit to wail her woe,
And I myself am all alone;
  Why dost thou weep? why dost thou wail,
  And knowest not yet what thou dost ail?

Come, little wretch! Ah, silly heart!
Mine only joy, what can I more?
If there be any wrong thy smart,
That may the destinies implore,
  'Twas I, I say, against my will:
  I wail the time, but be thou still.

And dost thou smile? Oh, thy sweet face!
Would God Himself He might thee see!
No doubt thou wouldst soon purchase grace,
I know right well, for thee and me:
  But come to mother, babe, and play,
  For father false is fled away.

Sweet boy, if it by fortune chance
Thy father home again to send,
If death do strike me with his lance,

Yet may'st thou me to him commend.
  If any ask thy mother's name,
  Tell how by love she purchased blame.

Then will his gentle heart soon yield;
I know him of a noble mind;
Although a lion in the field,
A lamb in town thou shalt him find:
  Ask blessing, babe, be not afraid!
  His sugared words hath me betrayed.

Then may'st thou joy and be right glad,
Although in woe I seem to moan;
Thy father is no rascal lad,
A noble youth of blood and bone:
  His glancing looks, if he once smile,
  Right honest women may beguile.

Come, little boy, and rock asleep!
Sing lullaby, and be thou still!
I, that can do nought else but weep,
Will sit by thee and wail my fill:
  God bless my babe, and lullaby,
  From this thy father's quality.

Magnolia Avenue

The name of the street was Magnolia Avenue,
but there were never any magnolias on it.
In the spring it was muddy.
Snot-nosed Dotty lived next door.
Wearing rubber boots, she waded
in the wet brown ooze, called out to me,
'Come on in, the water's fine.'
There was beautiful thick mud that morning
all over my stockings.
My mother scolded, called me away inside.

I climbed the stairway from the front hallway
to slide down the banisters all afternoon,
once, twice, a dozen, twenty times.
'You'll hurt yourself,' my mother called, grumbling.
'You'll ruin your flowered panties.'

I fell asleep playing with paper dolls.

In the evening after supper
I stood by the kitchen window eating cake
looking across at the window of Dotty's house.
Dotty's mother had black lace curtains.
They were drawn tight. Nobody looked out.
'Come away from the window,' Mother said.
'Someone will think you're spying.'

I never saw the inside of that room
and it was years before I saw magnolias.

[Epitaph]

Underneath this sable hearse
Lies the subject of all verse:
Sidney's sister, Pembroke's mother:
Death, ere thou hast slain another,
Fair and learned and good as she,
Time shall throw a dart at thee.

Marble piles let no man raise
To her name for after days;
Some kind woman born as she,
Reading this, like Niobe,
Shall turn marble, and become
Both her mourner and her tomb.

from *Aurora Leigh, Book 1*

I, writing thus, am still what men call young;
I have not so far left the coasts of life
To travel inward, that I cannot hear
That murmur of the outer Infinite
Which unweaned babies smile at in their sleep
When wondered at for smiling; not so far,
But still I catch my mother at her post
Beside the nursery door, with finger up,
'Hush, hush — here's too much noise!' while her sweet eyes
Leap forward, taking part against her word
In the child's riot. Still I sit and feel
My father's slow hand, when she had left us both,
Stroke out my childish curls across his knee,
And hear Assunta's daily jest (she knew
He liked it better than a better jest)
Inquire how many golden scudi went
To make such ringlets. O my father's hand,
Stroke heavily, heavily the poor hair down,
Draw, press the child's head closer to thy knee!
I'm still too young, too young, to sit alone.

I write. My mother was a Florentine,
Whose rare blue eyes were shut from seeing me
When scarcely I was four years old, my life
A poor spark snatched up from a failing lamp
Which went out therefore. She was weak and frail;
She could not bear the joy of giving life,
The mother's rapture slew her. If her kiss
Had left a longer weight upon my lips
It might have steadied the uneasy breath,

And reconciled and fraternised my soul
With the new order. As it was, indeed,
I felt a mother-want about the world,
And still went seeking, like a bleating lamb
Left out at night in shutting up the fold, –
As restless as a nest-deserted bird
Grown chill through something being away, though what
It knows not. I, Aurora Leigh, was born
To make my father sadder, and myself
Not overjoyous, truly. Women know
The way to rear up children (to be just),
They know a simple, merry, tender knack
Of tying sashes, fitting baby-shoes,
And stringing pretty words that make no sense,
And kissing full sense into empty words,
Which things are corals to cut life upon,
Although such trifles: children learn by such,
Love's holy earnest in a pretty play
And get not over-early solemnised,
But seeing, as in a rose-bush, Love Divine
Which burns and hurts not, – not a single bloom, –
Become aware and unafraid of Love.
Such good do mothers. Fathers love as well
– Mine did, I know, – but still with heavier brains,
And wills more consciously responsible,
And not as wisely, since less foolishly;
So mothers have God's licence to be missed . . .

from *Isobel's Child*

To rest the weary nurse has gone:
      An eight day watch watched she,
  Still rocking beneath sun and moon
      The baby on her knee,
  Till Isobel its mother said
'The fever waneth – wend to bed,
For now the watch comes round to me.'
  Then wearily the nurse did throw
      Her pallet in the darkest place
Of that sick room, and slept and dreamed:
  For, as the gusty wind did blow
      The night-lamp's flare across her face,
She saw, or seemed to see, but dreamed,
  That the poplars tall on the opposite hill,
The seven tall poplars on the hill,
Did clasp the setting sun until
His rays dropped from him, pined and still
  As blossoms in frost,
Till he waned and paled, so weirdly crossed,
To the colour of moonlight which doth pass
Over the dank ridged churchyard grass.
The poplars held the sun, and he
The eyes of the nurse that they should not see
 – Not for a moment, the babe on her knee,
Though she shuddered to feel that it grew to be
Too chill, and lay too heavily.

She only dreamed; for all the while
  'Twas Lady Isobel that kept
  The little baby: and it slept

Fast, warm, as if its mother's smile,
Laden with love's dewy weight,
And red as rose of Harpocrate,
Dropped upon its eyelids, pressed
Lashes to cheek in a sealed rest.

And more and more smiled Isobel
To see the baby sleep so well –
She knew not that she smiled.
Against the lattice, dull and wild
Drive the heavy, droning drops,
  Drop by drop, the sound being one;
As momently time's segments fall
On the ear of God, who hears through all
  Eternity's unbroken monotone:
And more and more smiled Isobel
To see the baby sleep so well –
She knew not that she smiled.
The wind in intermission stops
  Down in the beechen forest,
      Then cries aloud
  As one at the sorest,
      Self-stung, self-driven,
And rises up to its very tops,
Stiffening erect the branches bowed,
  Dilating with a tempest-soul
The trees that with their dark hands break
Through their own outline, and heavy roll
  Shadows as massive as clouds in heaven
      Across the castle lake.
And more and more smiled Isobel
To see the baby sleep so well;
She knew not that she smiled;
She knew not that the storm was wild;

Through the uproar drear she could not hear
The castle clock which struck anear –
She heard the low, light breathing of her child.

O sight for wondering look!
While the external nature broke
Into such abandonment,
While the very mist, heart-rent
By the lightning, seemed to eddy
Against nature, with a din, –
A sense of silence and of steady
Natural calm appeared to come
From things without, and enter in
The human creature's room.

So motionless she sate,
   The babe asleep upon her knees,
You might have dreamed their souls had gone
Away to things inanimate,
In such to live, in such to moan;
And that their bodies had ta'en back,
   In mystic change, all silences
That cross the sky in cloudy rack,
Or dwell beneath the reedy ground
In waters safe from their own sound:
         Only she wore
The deepening smile I named before,
And *that* a deepening love expressed;
And who at once can love and rest?

In sooth the smile that then was keeping
Watch upon the baby sleeping,
   Floated with its tender light
Downward, from the drooping eyes,
Upward, from the lips apart,
   Over cheeks which had grown white

With an eight-day weeping:
All smiles come in such a wise
Where tears shall fall or have of old –
Like northern lights that fill the heart
Of heaven in sign of cold.

Motionless she sate.
Her hair had fallen by its weight
On each side of her smile and lay
Very blackly on the arm
Where the baby nestled warm,
Pale as baby carved in stone
Seen by glimpses of the moon
Up a dark cathedral aisle:
But, through the storm, no moonbeam fell
Upon the child of Isobel –
Perhaps you saw it by the ray
Alone of her still smile. . . .

Waiting

'O come, O come,' the mother pray'd
   And hush'd her babe: 'let me behold
Once more thy stately form array'd
   Like autumn woods in green and gold!

'I see thy brethren come and go;
   Thy peers in stature, and in hue
Thy rivals. Some like monarchs glow
   With richest purple: some are blue

'As skies that tempt the swallow back;
   Or red as, seen o'er wintry seas,
The star of storm; or barr'd with black
   And yellow, like the April bees.

'Come they and go! I heed not, I.
   Yet others hail their advent, cling
All trustful to their side, and fly
   Safe in their gentle piloting

'To happy homes on heath or hill,
   By park or river. Still I wait
And peer into the darkness: still
   Thou com'st not – I am desolate.

'Hush! hark! I see a towering form!
   From the dim distance slowly roll'd
It rocks like lilies in a storm,
   And O, its hues are green and gold:

'It comes, it comes! Ah rest is sweet,
   And there is rest, my babe, for us!'
She ceased, as at her very feet
   Stopp'd the St John's Wood omnibus.

Motherhood

She laid it where the sunbeams fall
Unscann'd upon the broken wall.
Without a tear, without a groan,
She laid it near a mighty stone,
Which some rude swain had haply cast
Thither in sport, long ages past,
And Time with mosses had o'erlaid,
And fenced with many a tall grass blade,
And all about bid roses bloom
And violets shed their soft perfume.
There, in its cool and quiet bed,
She set her burden down and fled:
Nor flung, all eager to escape,
One glance upon the perfect shape
That lay, still warm and fresh and fair,
But motionless and soundless there.

No human eye had mark'd her pass
Across the linden-shadow'd grass
Ere yet the minster clock chimed seven:
Only the innocent bird of heaven –
The magpie, and the rook whose nest
Swings as the elm tree waves his crest –
And the lithe cricket, and the hoar
And huge-limb'd hound that guards the door,
Look'd on when, as a summer wind
That, passing, leaves no trace behind,
All unapparell'd, barefoot all,
She ran to that old ruin'd wall,
To leave upon the chill dank earth

(For ah! she never knew its worth)
'Mid hemlock rank, and fern and ling,
And dews of night, that precious thing.

   And there it might have lain forlorn
From morn till eve, from eve to morn:
But that, by some wild impulse led,
The mother, ere she turn'd and fled,
One moment stood erect and high;
Then pour'd into the silent sky
A cry so jubilant, so strange,
That Alice – as she strove to range
Her rebel ringlets at her glass –
Sprang up and gazed across the grass;
Shook back those curls so fair to see,
Clapp'd her soft hands in childish glee;
And shriek'd – her sweet face all aglow,
   Her very limbs with rapture shaking –
   'My hen has laid an egg, I know;
   And only hear the noise she's making!'

On the Brink

I watch'd her as she stooped to pluck
  A wildflower in her hair to twine;
And wish'd that it had been my luck
  To call her mine.

Anon I heard her rate with mad
  Mad words her babe within its cot;
And felt particularly glad
  That it had not.

I knew (such subtle brains have men)
  That she was uttering what she shouldn't;
And thought that I would chide, and then
  I thought I wouldn't:

Who could have gazed upon that face,
  Those pouting coral lips, and chided?
A Rhadamanthus, in my place,
  Had done as I did:

For ire wherewith our bosoms glow
  Is chain'd there oft by Beauty's spell;
And, more than that, I did not know
  The widow well.

So the harsh phrase pass'd unreproved.
  Still mute – (O brothers, was it sin?) –
I drank, unutterably moved,
  Her beauty in:

And to myself I murmur'd low,
  As on her upturn'd face and dress
The moonlight fell, 'Would she say No,
  By chance, or Yes?'

She stood so calm, so like a ghost
  Betwixt me and that magic moon,
That I already was almost
  A finish'd coon.

But when she caught adroitly up
  And sooth'd with smiles her little daughter;
And gave it, if I'm right, a sup
  Of barley-water;

And, crooning still the strange sweet lore
  Which only mothers' tongues can utter,
Snow'd with deft hand the sugar o'er
  Its bread-and-butter;

And kiss'd it clingingly – (Ah, why
  Don't women do these things in private?) –
I felt that if I lost her, I
  Should not survive it:

And from my mouth the words nigh flew –
  The past, the future, I forgat 'em:
'Oh! if you'd kiss me as you do
  That thankless atom!'

But this thought came ere I spake,
  And froze the sentence on my lips:
'They err who marry wives that make
  Those little slips.'

It came like some familiar rhyme,
  Some copy to my boyhood set;
And that's perhaps the reason I'm
  Unmarried yet.

Would she have own'd how pleased she was,
  And told her love with widow's pride?
I never found that out, because
  I never tried.

Be kind to babes and beasts and birds:
  Hearts may be hard, though lips are coral;
And angry words are angry words:
  And that's the moral.

'My Mother Saw a Dancing Bear'

My mother saw a dancing bear
By the schoolyard, a day in June.
The keeper stood with chain and bar
And whistle-pipe, and played a tune.

And bruin lifted up its head
And lifted up its dusty feet,
And all the children laughed to see
It caper in the summer heat.

They watched as for the Queen it died.
They watched it march. They watched it halt.
They heard the keeper as he cried,
'Now, roly-poly!' 'Somersault!'

And then, my mother said, there came
The keeper with a begging-cup,
The bear with burning coat of fur,
Shaming the laughter to a stop.

They paid a penny for the dance,
But what they saw was not the show;
Only, in bruin's aching eyes,
Far-distant forests, and the snow.

'What Has Happened to Lulu?'

What has happened to Lulu, mother?
  What has happened to Lu?
There's nothing in bed but an old rag-doll
  And by its side a shoe.

Why is her window wide, mother,
  The curtain flapping free,
And only a circle on the dusty shelf
  Where her money-box used to be?

Why do you turn your head, mother,
  And why do the tear-drops fall?
And why do you crumple that note on the fire
  And say it is nothing at all?

I woke to voices late last night,
  I heard an engine roar.
Why do you tell me the things I heard
  Were a dream and nothing more?

I heard somebody cry, mother,
  In anger or in pain,
But now I ask you why, mother,
  You say it was a gust of rain.

Why do you wander about as though
  You don't know what to do?
What has happened to Lulu, mother?
  What has happened to Lu?

An Elegy on a Maiden Name

Adieu, dear name, which birth and nature gave –
Lo, at the altar I've interred dear CAVE;
For there it fell, expired, and found a grave.

Forgive, dear spouse, this ill-timed tear or two,
They are not meant in disrespect to you;
I hope the name which you have lately given
Was kindly meant, and sent to me by heaven.
But ah! the loss of CAVE I must deplore,
For that dear name the tenderest mother bore.
With that she passed full forty years of life,
Adorned the important character of wife:
Then meet for bliss from earth to heaven retired,
With holy zeal and true devotion fired.

In me what blessed my father may you find,
A wife domestic, virtuous, meek, and kind.
What blessed my mother may I meet in you,
A friend and husband – faithful, wise, and true.

Then be our voyage prosperous or adverse,
No keen upbraiding shall our tongues rehearse;
But mutually we'll brave against the storm,
Remembering still for helpmates we were born.
Then let rough torrents roar or skies look dark,
If love commands the helm which guides our bark,
No shipwreck will we fear, but to the end
Each find in each a just, unshaken friend.

Written a Few Hours Before the Birth of a Child

My God, prepare me for that hour
  When most thy aid I want;
Uphold me by thy mighty power,
  Nor let my spirits faint.

I ask not life, I ask not ease,
  But patience to submit
To what shall best thy goodness please,
  Then come what thou seest fit.

Come pain, or agony, or death,
  If such the will divine;
With joy shall I give up my breath,
  If resignation's mine.

One wish to name I'd humbly dare,
  If death thy pleasure be:
O may the harmless babe I bear
  Haply expire with me.

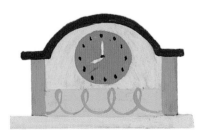

Sonnet

To a friend who asked me how it felt when the nurse first presented my infant to me

Charles! my slow heart was only sad when first
   I scanned that face of feeble infancy:
For dimly on my thoughtful spirit burst
   All I had been, and all my child might be!
But when I saw it on its mother's arm,
   And hanging at her bosom (she the while
   Bent o'er its features with a tearful smile)
Then I was thrilled and melted, and most warm
Impressed a father's kiss: and all beguiled
   Of dark remembrance and presageful fear,
   I seemed to see an angel-form appear –
'Twas even thine, beloved woman mild!
   So for the mother's sake the child was dear,
And dearer was the mother for the child.

A Child's Evening Prayer

Ere on my bed my limbs I lay,
God grant me peace my prayers to say:
O God! preserve my mother dear
In strength and health for many a year;
And, O! preserve my father too,
And may I pay him reverence due;
And may I my best thoughts employ
To be my parents' hope and joy;
And O! preserve my brothers both
From evil doings and from sloth,
And may we always love each other,
Our friends, our father, and our mother:
And still, O Lord, to me impart
An innocent and grateful heart,
That after my great sleep I may
Awake to thy eternal day! Amen.

'The Singing Kettle and the Purring Cat'

The singing kettle and the purring cat,
The gentle breathing of the cradled babe,
The silence of the mother's love-bright eye,
And tender smile answering its smile of sleep.

The Mother

Full oft beside some gorgeous fane
  The youngling heifer bleeds and dies;
Her life-blood issuing forth amain,
  While wreaths of incense climb the skies.

The mother wanders all around,
  Thro' shadowy groves and lightsome glade;
Her footmarks on the yielding ground
  Will prove what anxious quest she made.

The stall where late her darling lay
  She visits oft with eager look;
In restless movements wastes the day,
  And fills with cries each neighb'ring nook.

She roams along the willowy copse,
  Where purest waters softly gleam;
But ne'er a leaf or blade she crops,
  Nor couches by the gliding stream.

No youthful kine, tho' fresh and fair,
  Her vainly searching eyes engage;
No pleasant fields relieve her care,
  No murmuring streams her grief assuage.

On the Receipt of My Mother's Picture Out of Norfolk, The Gift of My Cousin Ann Bodham

Oh that those lips had language! Life has passed
With me but roughly since I heard thee last.
Those lips are thine – thy own sweet smiles I see,
The same that oft in childhood solaced me;
Voice only fails, else, how distinct they say,
'Grieve not, my child, chase all thy fears away!'
The meek intelligence of those dear eyes
(Blest be the art that can immortalise,
The art that baffles Time's tyrannic claim
To quench it) here shines on me still the same.
  Faithful remembrancer of one so dear,
O welcome guest, though unexpected, here!
Who bidd'st me honour with an artless song,
Affectionate, a mother lost so long:
I will obey, not willingly alone,
But gladly, as the precept were her own;
And, while that face renews my filial grief,
Fancy shall weave a charm for my relief –
Shall steep me in Elysian reverie,
A momentary dream, that thou art she.

My mother! when I learned that thou wast dead,
Say, wast thou conscious of the tears I shed?
Hovered thy spirit o'er thy sorrowing son,
Wretch even then, life's journey just begun?
Perhaps thou gavest me, though unseen, a kiss;
Perhaps a tear, if souls can weep in bliss –
Ah that maternal smile! It answers – Yes.
I heard the bell tolled on thy burial day.
I saw the hearse that bore thee slow away,
And, turning from my nursery window, drew
A long, long sigh, and wept a last adieu!
But was it such? – It was. – Where thou art gone
Adieus and farewells are a sound unknown.
May I but meet thee on that peaceful shore,
The parting sound shall pass my lips no more!
Thy maidens grieved themselves at my concern,
Oft gave me promise of a quick return.
What ardently I wished, I long believed,
And, disappointed still, was still deceived;
By disappointment every day beguiled,
Dupe of tomorrow, even from a child.
Thus many a sad tomorrow came and went,
Till, all my stock of infant sorrow spent,
I learned at last submission to my lot;
But, though I less deplored thee, ne'er forgot.

Where once we dwelt our name is heard no more,
Children not thine have trod my nursery floor;
And where the gardener, Robin, day by day,
Drew me to school along the public way,
Delighted with my bauble coach, and wrapped
In scarlet mantle warm, and velvet capped,
'Tis now become a history little known
That once we called the pastoral house our own:
Short-lived possession! But the record fair

That memory keeps of all thy kindness there,
Still outlives many a storm that has effaced
A thousand other themes less deeply traced.
Thy nightly visits to my chamber made,
That thou mightest know me safe and warmly laid;
Thy morning bounties ere I left my home,
The biscuit or confectionary plum;
The fragrant waters on my cheeks bestowed
By thy own hand, till fresh they shone and glowed;
All this, and more endearing still than all,
Thy constant flow of love that knew no fall,
Ne'er roughened by those cataracts and brakes
That humour interposed too often makes;
All this still legible in memory's page,
And still to be so, to my latest age,
Adds joy to duty, makes me glad to pay
Such honours to thee as my numbers may;
Perhaps a frail memorial, but sincere,
Not scorned in heaven, though little noticed here.
   Could Time, his flight reversed, restore the hours
When, playing with thy vesture's tissued flowers,
The violet, the pink, and jessamine,
I pricked them into paper with a pin
(And thou wast happier than myself the while,
Would'st softly speak, and stroke my head, and smile):
Could those few pleasant hours again appear,
Might one wish bring them, would I wish them here?
I would not trust my heart – the dear delight
Seems so to be desired, perhaps I might.
But no – what here we call our life is such,
So little to be loved, and thou so much,
That I should ill requite thee to constrain
Thy unbound spirit into bonds again.
   Thou, as a gallant bark from Albion's coast

(The storms all weathered, and the ocean crossed)
Shoots into port at some well-havened isle,
Where spices breathe and brighter seasons smile,
There sits quiescent on the floods that show
Her beauteous form reflected clear below,
While airs impregnated with incense play
Around her, fanning light her streamers gay;
So thou, with sails how swift, hast reached the shore
'Where tempests never beat, nor billows roar,'
And thy loved consort on the dangerous tide
Of life, long since, has anchored at thy side.
But me, scarce hoping to attain that rest,
Always from port withheld, always distressed –
Me howling winds drive devious, tempest tossed,
Sails ripped, seams opening wide, and compass lost,
And day by day some current's thwarting force
Sets me more distant from a prosperous course.
But oh the thought, that thou art safe, and he!
That thought is joy, arrive what may to me.
My boast is not that I deduce my birth
From loins enthroned, and rulers of the earth;

But higher far my proud pretensions rise –
The son of parents passed into the skies.
And now, farewell – Time, unrevoked, has run
His wonted course, yet what I wished is done.
By contemplation's help, not sought in vain,
I seem to have lived my childhood o'er again;
To have renewed the joys that once were mine,
Without the sin of violating thine:
And, while the wings of fancy still are free,
And I can view this mimic show of thee,
Time has but half succeeded in his theft –
Thyself removed, thy power to soothe me left.

Mary, Mary

Mary, Mary, quite contrary,
How does your garden grow?
'I live with my brat in a high-rise flat,
So how in the world would I know.'

The Price of Debauchery

My mother said, 'There are no joys
In ever kissing silly boys.
Just one small *kiss* and one small squeeze
Can land you with some foul disease.'

'But Mum, d'you mean from just a *kiss*?'

'You know quite well my meaning, miss.'

Last week when coming home from school
I clean forgot Mum's golden rule
I let Tom Young, that handsome louse,
Steal one small kiss behind my house.

Oh, woe is me! I've paid the price!
I should have listened to advice.
My Mum was right one hundredfold!
I've caught Tom's horrid runny cold!

Amantium Irae Amoris Redintegratio

In going to my naked bed as one that would have slept,
I heard a wife sing to her child, that long before had wept.
She sighed sore and sang full sweet to bring the babe to rest,
That would not rest, but cried still, in sucking at her breast.
She was full weary of her watch and grieved with her child;
She rocked it and rated it until on her it smiled.
Then did she say, 'Now have I found the proverb true to
    prove,
The falling out of faithful friends is the renewing of love.'

Then took I paper, pen and ink, this proverb for to write,
In register for to remain of such a worthy wight.
As she proceeded thus in song unto her little brat,
Much matter uttered she of weight, in place whereas she sat;
And proved plain there was no beast, nor creature bearing life,
Could well be known to live in love without discord and
    strife.
Then kissed she her little babe and sware by God above,
'The falling out of faithful friends is the renewing of love.'

She said that neither king, ne prince, ne lord could live
    aright,
Until their puissance they did prove, their manhood and their
    might;
When manhood shall be matched so that fear can take no
    place,
Then weary works make warriors each other to embrace,
And leave their force that failed them, which did consume the
    rout,
That might before have lived their time and nature out.

Then did she sing as one that thought no man could her
    reprove,
'The falling out of faithful friends is the renewing of love.'

She said she saw no fish, ne fowl, ne beast within her haunt
That met a stranger in their kind, but could give it a taunt.
Since flesh might not endure, but rest must wrath succeed,
And force the fight to fall to play in pasture where they feed,
So noble nature can well end the works she hath begun,
And bridle well that will not cease, her tragedy in some.
Thus in her song she oft rehearsed, as did her well behove,
'The falling out of faithful friends is the renewing of love.'

'I marvel much, perdy!' (quoth she) 'for to behold the rout,
To see man, woman, boy and beast, to toss the world about.
Some kneel, some crouch, some beck, some check, and
    some can smoothly smile,
And some embrace others in arms, and there think many a
    wile.
Some stand aloof at cap and knee, some humble and some
    stout,
Yet are they never friends indeed until they once fall out.'
Thus ended she her song, and said, before she did remove,
'The falling out of faithful friends is the renewing of love.'

[The Punishment of Niobe]

She falleth on the corpses cold and, taking no regard,
Bestowed her kisses on her sons as whom she afterward
Did know she never more should kiss. From whom she lifting
   tho
Her blue and bruised arms to heaven, said: 'O, thou cruel foe
Latona, feed, yea feed thyself, I say, upon my woe,
And overgorge thy stomach, yea, and glut thy cruel heart
With these my present painful pangs of bitter-griping smart.
In corpses seven I seven times dead am carried to my grave.
Rejoice, thou foe, and triumph now in that thou seemest to
   have
The upper hand. What? Upper hand? No, no, it is not so.
As wretched as my case doth seem, yet have I left me mo
Than thou for all thy happiness canst of thine own account.
Even after all these corpses, yet I still do thee surmount.'
Upon the end of these same words the twanging of the string
In letting of the arrow fly was clearly heard: which thing
Made everyone save Niobe afraid. Her heart was so
With sorrow hardened that she grew more bold. Her
   daughters tho
Were standing all mourning weed and hanging hair before
Their brothers' coffins. One of them, in pulling from the
   sore
An arrow sticking in his heart, sank down upon her brother
With mouth to mouth, and so did yield her fleeting ghost.
   Another
In comforting the wretched case and sorrow of her mother
Upon the sudden held her peace. She stricken was within
With double wound, which caused her her talking for to blin

And shut her mouth: but first her ghost was gone. One, all in
    vain
Attempting for to escape by flight was in her flying slain.
Another on her sister's corpse doth tumble down stark dead.
This quakes and trembles piteously, and she doth hide her
    head.
And when that six with sundry wounds dispatched were and
    gone,
At last as yet remained one; and, for to save that one,
Her mother with her body whole did cling about her fast,
And wrying her did over her her garments wholly cast,
And cried out: 'O leave me one: this little one yet save:
Of many but this only one the least of all I crave.'
But whiles she prayed, for whom she prayed was killed.
    Then down she sat
Bereft of all her children quite, and drawing to her fate,
Among her daughters and her sons and husband newly dead.
Her cheeks waxed hard; the air could stir no hair upon her
    head;
The colour of her face was dim and clearly void of blood,
And sadly under open lids her eyes unmoved stood.
In all her body was no life, for even her very tongue
And palate of her mouth was hard, and each to other clung.
Her pulses ceased for to beat; her neck did cease to bow;
Her arms to stir, her feet to go, all power forewent as now;
And into stone her very womb and bowels also bind.
But yet she wept, and, being hoist by force of whirling wind,
Was carried into Phrygia. There upon a mountain's top
She weepeth still in stone. From stone the dreary tears do
    drop . . .

In Childbed

In the middle of the night
Mother's spirit came and spoke to me,
    Looking weariful and white –
As 'twere untimely news she broke to me.

'O my daughter, joyed are you
To own the weetless child you mother there;
    "Men may search the wide world through,"
You think, "nor find so fair another there!"

'Dear, this midnight time unwombs
Thousands just as rare and beautiful;
    Thousands whom High Heaven foredooms
To be as bright, as good, as dutiful.

'Source of ecstatic hopes and fears
And innocent maternal vanity,
    Your fond exploit but shapes for tears
New thoroughfares in sad humanity.

'Yet as you dream, so dreamt I
When life stretched forth its morning ray to me;
    Other views for by and by!' . . .
Such strange things did my mother say to me.

The Christening

Whose child is this they bring
  Into the aisle? –
At so superb a thing
The congregation smile
And turn their heads awhile.

Its eyes are blue and bright,
  Its cheeks like rose;
Its simple robes unite
Whitest of calicoes
With lawn, and satin bows.

A pride in the human race
  At this paragon
Of mortals, lights each face
While the old rite goes on;
But ah, they are shocked anon.

What girl is she who peeps
  From the gallery stair,
Smiles palely, redly weeps,
With feverish furtive air
As though not fitly there?

'I am the baby's mother;
  This gem of the race
The decent fain would smother,
And for my deep disgrace
I am bidden to leave the place.'

'Where is the baby's father?' —
    'In the woods afar.
He says there is none he'd rather
Meet under moon or star
Than me, of all that are.

'To clasp me in lovelike weather,
    Wish fixing when,
He says: To be together
At will, just now and then,
Makes him the blest of men;

'But chained and doomed for life
    To slovening
As vulgar man and wife,
He says, is another thing:
Yea, sweet Love's sepulchring!'

News for Her Mother

One mile more is
Where your door is,
   Mother mine! –
Harvest's coming,
Mills are strumming,
   Apples fine,
And the cider made to-year will be as wine.

Yet, not viewing
What's a-doing
   Here around
Is it thrills me,
And so fills me
   That I bound
Like a ball or leaf or lamb along the ground.

Tremble not now
At your lot now,
   Silly soul!
Hosts have sped them
Quick to wed them,
   Great and small,
Since the first two sighing half-hearts made a whole.

Yet I wonder,
Will it sunder
   Her from me?
Will she guess that
I said 'Yes,' – that
   His I'd be,
Ere I thought she might not see him as I see!

Old brown gable,
Granary, stable,
Here you are!
O my mother,
Can another
Ever bar
Mine from my heart, make thy nearness seem afar?

To His Mother

There was a battle fought of late,
  Yet was the slaughter small;
The strife was whether I should write,
  Or send nothing at all.
Of one side were the captains' names
  Short Time and Little Skill;
One fought alone against them both,
  Whose name was Great Good-will.
Short Time enforced me in a strait,
  And bade me hold my hand;
Small Skill also withstood desire
  My writing to withstand.
But Great Good-will, in show though small,
  To write encouraged me,
And to the battle held on still,
  No common thing to see.
Thus 'gan these busy warriors three
  Between themselves to fight
As valiantly as though they had
  Been of much greater might.
Till Fortune, that unconstant dame,
  Which rules such things alway,
Did cause the weaker part in fight
  To bear the greater sway.
And then the victor caused me,
  However was my skill,
To write these verses unto you
  To show my great good-will.

The Painting Lesson

'What's THAT, dear?'
asked the new teacher.

'It's Mummy,' I replied.

'But mums aren't green and orange!
You really haven't TRIED.
You don't just paint in SPLODGES
– You're old enough to know
You need to THINK before you work…
Now – have another go.'

She helped me draw two arms and legs,
A face with sickly smile,
A rounded body, dark brown hair,
A hat – and, in a while,
She stood back (with her face bright pink):
'That's SO much better – don't you think?'

But she turned white
At ten to three
When an orange-green blob
Collected me.

'Hi, Mum!'

To My Mother

If e'er for human bliss or woe
I feel the sympathetic glow;
If e'er my heart has learned to know
        The generous wish or prayer;
Who sowed the germ, with tender hand?
Who marked its infant leaves expand?
        My mother's fostering care.

And if *one* flower of charms refined
May grace the garden of my mind,
        'Twas she who nursed it there;
    She loved to cherish and adorn
        Each blossom of the soil;
    To banish every weed and thorn,
        That oft opposed her toil.

And, oh! if e'er I've sighed to claim
The palm, the living palm of fame,
        The glowing wreath of praise;
If e'er I've wished the glittering stores
That fortune on her favourite pours,
'Twas but that wealth and fame, if mine,
Round *thee*, with streaming rays might shine,
        And gild thy sun-bright days.

Yet not that splendour, pomp, and power,
Might then irradiate every hour;
For these, my mother, well I know,
On thee no rapture could bestow;
But could thy bounty, warm and kind,
Be, like thy wishes, unconfined,

And fall, as manna from the skies,
And bid a train of blessings rise,
      Diffusing joy and peace;
The tear-drop, grateful, pure and bright,
For thee would beam with softer light
Than all the diamond's crystal rays,
Than all the emerald's lucid blaze;
And joys of heaven would thrill thy heart,
To bid one bosom-grief depart,
      One tear, one sorrow cease!

Then, oh! may heaven, that loves to bless,
Bestow the power to cheer distress;
Make thee its minister below,
To light the cloudy path of woe;
To visit the deserted cell
Where indigence is doomed to dwell;
To raise, when drooping to the earth,
The blossoms of neglected worth;
And round, with liberal hand, dispense
The sunshine of beneficence.

But ah, if fate should still deny
Delights like these, too rich and high;
If grief and pain thy steps assail
In life's remote and wintry vale;
Then, as the wild Aeolian lyre
      Complains with soft, entrancing number
When the loud storm awakes the wire,
      And bids enchantment cease to slumber;
So filial love, with soothing voice,
E'en then shall teach me to rejoice:
E'en then shall sweeter, milder sound,
When sorrow's tempest raves around;
While dark misfortune's gales destroy
The frail mimosa-buds of hope and joy!

To Dianeme. A Ceremony in Gloucester

I'll to thee a simnel bring
'Gainst thou goest a-Mothering,
So that, when she blesseth thee,
Half that blessing thou'lt give me.

Brother

I had a little brother
And I brought him to my mother
And I said I want another
Little brother for a change.

But she said don't be a bother
So I took him to my father
And I said this little bother
Of a brother's very strange.

But he said one little brother
Is exactly like another
And every little brother
Misbehaves a bit he said.

So I took the little bother
From my mother and my father
And I put the little bother
Of a brother back to bed.

Mother to Son

Well, son, I'll tell you:
Life for me ain't been no crystal stair.
It's had tacks in it,
And splinters,
And boards torn up,
And places with no carpet on the floor —
Bare.
But all the time
I'se been a-climbin' on,
And reachin' landin's,

And turnin' corners,
And sometimes goin' in the dark
Where there ain't been no light.
So, boy, don't you turn back.
Don't you set down on the steps
'Cause you finds it's kinder hard.
Don't you fall now
For I'se still goin', honey,
I'se still climbin',
And life for me ain't been no crystal stair.

A Pastoral Song

My mother bids me bind my hair
  With bands of rosy hue,
Tie up my sleeves with ribbons rare,
  And lace my bodice blue.

'For why,' she cries, 'sit still and weep
  While others dance and play?'
Alas! I scarce can go or creep
  While Lubin is away.

'Tis sad to think the days are gone
  When those we love were near;
I sit upon this mossy stone,
  And sigh when none can hear.

And while I spin my flaxen thread,
  And sing my simple lay,
The village seems asleep, or dead,
  Now Lubin is away.

Clothes

My mother keeps on telling me
When she was in her teens
She wore quite different clothes from mine
And hadn't heard of jeans,

T-shirts, no hats, and dresses that
Reach far above our knees.
I laughed at first and then I thought
One day my kids will tease

And scoff at what *I'm* wearing now.
What will *their* fashions be?
I'd give an awful lot to know,
To look ahead and see.

Girls dressed like girls perhaps once more
And boys no longer half
Resembling us. Oh, what's in store
To make *our* children laugh?

To My Mother at 73

Will you always catch me unaware,
Find me fumbling, holding back? You claim
Little, ask ordinary things, don't dare
Utter endearments much but speak my name
As if you hoped to find a child there,
There on the phone, the same

You tried to quiet. You seem to want the years
Wrapped up and tossed away. You need me to
Prove you are needed. Can you sense the tears
So pent up, so afraid of hurting you?
Must we both fumble not to show our fears
Of holding back our pain, our kindness too?

A Mother's Love

I love thee, I love thee, and life will depart
Ere thy mother forget thee, sweet child of her heart;
Yea, death's shadows only my memory can dim,
For thou'rt dearer than life to me – Mary Achin.

I love thee, I love thee, and six years hath now fled
Since first on my bosom I pillowed thy head;
Since I first did behold thee in sorrow and sin,
Thou sweet offspring of false love – my Mary Achin.

I love thee, I love thee, and twelve months hath now past,
My sweet child, since I gazed on thy fairy form last;
And our parting brought sorrow, known only to Him
Who can see through the heart's depths – my Mary Achin.

I love thee, I love thee, oh! when shalt thou rest
Thy sweet angel face on this heart-baring breast;
Thy last parting kiss lingers still on my chin,
Embalmed with a blessing from Mary Achin.

I love thee, I love thee, thy beauty and youth
Are spotless and pure as the fountain of truth;
Thou'rt my star in the night till daybreak begin,
And my sunshine by noontide – my Mary Achin.

I love thee, I love thee, wherever I go
Thou'rt shrined in my bosom in joy or in woe;
A murmuring music my fancy doth win,
'Tis the voice of my darling – Mary Achin.

I love thee, I love thee, is ever my lay,
I sigh it by night and I sing it by day;
Its chorus swells forth like the stern patriot's hymn,
Thrice hallowed with visions of Mary Achin.

I love thee, I love thee, though now far away
Thou'rt nearer and dearer to me every day;
Would they give me my choice – a nation to win –
I would not exchange with my Mary Achin.

To an Unborn Infant

Be still, sweet babe, no harm shall reach thee,
  Nor hurt thy yet unfinished form;
Thy mother's frame shall safely guard thee
  From this bleak, this beating storm.

Promised hope! expected treasure!
  Oh, how welcome to these arms!
Feeble, yet they'll fondly clasp thee,
  Shield thee from the least alarms.

Loved already, little blessing,
  Kindly cherished, though unknown,
Fancy forms thee sweet and lovely,
  Emblem of the rose unblown.

Though thy father is imprisoned,
  Wronged, forgotten, robbed of right,
I'll repress the rising anguish,
  Till thine eyes behold the light.

Start not, babe! the hour approaches
  That presents the gift of life;
Soon, too soon, thou'lt taste of sorrow
  In these realms of care and strife.

Share not thou a mother's feelings,
  Hope vouchsafes a pitying ray;
Though a gloom obscures the morning,
  Bright may shine the rising day.

Live, sweet babe, to bless thy father,
    When thy mother slumbers low;
Slowly lisp her name that loved him,
    Through a world of varied woe.

Learn, my child, the mournful story
    Of thy suffering mother's life;
Let thy father not forget her
    In a future, happier wife.

Babe of fondest expectation,
    Watch his wishes in his face;
What pleased in me may'st thou inherit,
    And supply my vacant place.

Whisper all the anguished moments
    That have wrung this anxious breast:
Say, I lived to give thee being,
    And retire to endless rest.

[A Defence of Eve]

Now Pontius Pilate is to judge the cause
Of faultless Jesus, who before him stands,
Who neither hath offended prince nor laws,
Although He now be brought in woeful bands.
O noble governor, make thou yet a pause:
Do not in innocent blood imbrue thy hands,
  But hear the words of thy most worthy wife,
  Who sends to thee to beg her Saviour's life.

Let barbarous cruelty far depart from thee,
And in true justice take affliction's part;
Open thine eyes, that thou the truth may'st see:
Do not the thing that goes against thy heart;
Condemn not Him that must thy Saviour be,
But view His holy life, His good desert.
  Let not us women glory in men's fall,
  Who had power given to overrule us all.

Till now your indiscretion sets us free
And makes our former faults much less appear:
Our mother Eve, who tasted of the tree,
Giving to Adam what she held most dear,
Was simply good, and had no power to see:
The aftercoming harm did not appear.
  The subtle serpent that our sex betrayed
  Before the Fall so sure a plot had laid

That undiscerning ignorance perceived
No guile nor craft that was by him intended;
For had she known of what we were bereaved,
To his request she had not condescended.

But she, poor soul, by cunning was deceived:
No hurt therein her harmless heart intended;
  For she alleged God's word, which he denies,
  That they should die, but even as gods be wise.

But surely Adam cannot be excused:
Her fault though great, yet he was most to blame:
What weakness offered, strength might have refused.
Being lord of all, the greater was his shame:
Although the serpent's craft had her abused,
God's holy word ought all his actions frame;
  For he was lord and king of all the earth
  Before poor Eve had either life or breath.

Who, being framed by God's eternal hand,
The perfect'st man that ever breathed on earth;
And from God's mouth received the strait command,
The breath whereof he knew was present death:
Yea, having power to rule both sea and land,
Yet with one apple won to lose that breath
  Which God had breathed on his beauteous face,
  Bringing us all in danger and disgrace.

And then to lay the fault on patience's back,
That we, poor women, must endure it all!
We know right well he did discretion lack,
Being not persuaded thereunto at all.
If Eve did err, it was for knowledge's sake;
The fruit, being fair, persuaded him to fall:
  No subtle serpent's falsehood did betray him;
  If he would eat it, who had power to stay him?

Not Eve, whose fault was only too much love,
Which made her give this present to her dear,
That what she tasted he likewise might prove,
Whereby his knowledge might become more clear:

He never sought her weakness to reprove
With those sharp words which he of God did hear.
    Yet men will boast of knowledge, which he took
    From Eve's fair hand, as from a learned book.

If any evil did in her remain,
Being made of him, he was the ground of all:
If one of many worlds could lay a stain
Upon our sex, and work so great a fall
To wretched man by Satan's subtle train,
What will so foul a fault amongst you all?
    Her weakness did the serpent's words obey,
    But you in malice God's dear Son betray . . .

The Natural Child

Let not the title of my verse offend,
  Nor let the prude contract her rigid brow;
That helpless innocence demands a friend,
  Virtue herself will cheerfully allow:

And should my pencil prove too weak to paint
  The ills attendant on the babe ere born,
Whose parents swerved from Virtue's mild restraint,
  Forgive the attempt, nor treat the muse with scorn.

Yon rural farm, where mirth was wont to dwell,
  Of melancholy now appears the seat;
Solemn and silent as the hermit's cell –
  Say what, my muse, has caused a change so great?

This hapless morn an infant first saw light,
  Whose innocence a better fate might claim
Than to be shunned as hateful to the sight,
  And banished soon as it receives a name.

No joy attends its entrance into life,
  No smile upon its mother's face appears.
She cannot smile, alas! she is no wife,
  But vents the sorrow of her heart in tears.

No father flies to clasp it to his breast,
  And bless the power that gave it to his arms;
To see his form, in miniature expressed,
  Or trace, with ecstasy, its mother's charms.

Unhappy babe! thy father is thy foe!
    Oft shall he wish thee numbered with the dead;
His crime entails on thee a load of woe,
    And sorrow heaps on thy devoted head.

Torn from its mother's breast, by shame or pride –
    No matter which – to hireling hands assigned;
A parent's tenderness when thus denied,
    Can it be thought its nurse is over-kind?

Too many like this infant we may see,
    Exposed, abandoned, helpless and forlorn;
Till death, misfortune's friend, has set them free
    From a rude world which gave them nought but scorn.

Too many mothers – horrid to relate!
    Soon as their infants breathe the vital air,
Deaf to their plaintive cries, their helpless state,
    Led on by shame, and driven by despair,

Fell murderers become – Here cease, my pen,
    And leave these wretched victims of despair;
But ah! what punishments await the men
    Who in such depths of misery plunge the fair?

Everybody's Mother

Of course
everybody's mother always and
so on…

Always never
loved you enough
or too smothering much.

Of course you were the Only One, your
mother
a machine
that shat out siblings, listen

everybody's mother
was the original Frigid-
aire Icequeen clunking out
the hardstuff in nuggets, mirror
slivers and ice-splinters that'd stick
in your heart.

Absolutely everyone's mother
was artistic when she was young.

Everyone's mother
was a perfumed presence with pearls, remote
white shoulders when she
bent over in her ball dress
to kiss you in your crib.

Everybody's mother slept with the butcher
for sausages to stuff you with.

Everyone's mother
mythologised herself. You got mixed up
between dragon's teeth and black market stockings.

Naturally
She failed to give you
Positive Feelings
about your own sorry
sprouting body (it was a bloody shame)

but she did
sit up all night sewing sequins
on your carnival costume

so you would have a good time

and she spat
on the corner of her hanky and scraped
at your mouth with sour lace till you squirmed
so you would look smart

And where
was your father all this time?
Away
at the war, or
in his office, or any-
way conspicuous for his
Absence, so

what if your mother did
float around above you
big as a barrage balloon
blocking out the light?

Nobody's mother can't not never do nothing right.

A Terrible Infant

I recollect a nurse call'd Ann
 Who carried me about the grass,
And one fine day a fine young man
 Came up, and kiss'd the pretty lass.
She did not make the least objection!
 Thinks I, *'Aha!*
 When I can talk I'll tell Mamma.'
 – And that's my earliest recollection.

To My Grandmother

(Suggested by a Picture by Mr Romney)

This relative of mine
Was she seventy and nine
    When she died?
By the canvas may be seen
How she looked at seventeen,
    As a bride.

Beneath a summer tree
As she sits, her reverie
    Has a charm;
Her ringlets are in taste, –
What an arm! and what a waist
    For an arm!

In bridal coronet,
Lace, ribbons, and *coquette*
    Falbala;
Were Romney's limning true,
What a lucky dog were you,
    Grandpapa!

Her lips were sweet as love, –
They are parting! Do they move?
    Are they dumb? –
Her eyes are blue, and beam
Beseechingly, and seem
    To say, 'Come.'

What funny fancy slips
From atween these cherry lips?
　　Whisper me,
Sweet deity, in paint,
What canon says I mayn't
　　Marry thee?

That good-for-nothing Time
Has a confidence sublime!
　　When I first
Saw this lady, in my youth,
Her winters had, forsooth,
　　Done their worst.

Her locks (as white as snow)
Once shamed the swarthy crow;
　　By and by
That fowl's avenging sprite
Set his cloven hoof for spite
　　In her eye.

Her rounded form was lean,
And her silk was bombazine: –
　　Well I wot,
With her needles would she sit,
And for hours would she knit, –
　　Would she not?

Ah, perishable clay!
Her charms had dropp'd away
　　One by one.
But if she heaved a sigh
With a burthen, it was 'Thy
　　Will be done.'

In travail, as in tears,
With the fardel of her years
　　Overprest, –
In mercy was she borne
Where the weary ones and worn
　　Are at rest.

I'm fain to meet you there, –
If as witching as you were,
　　Grandmamma!
This nether world agrees
That the better it must please
　　Grandpapa.

To His Mother, C.L.M.

In the dark womb where I began
My mother's life made me a man.
Through all the months of human birth
Her beauty fed my common earth.
I cannot see, nor breathe, nor stir,
But through the death of some of her.

Down in the darkness of the grave
She cannot see the life she gave.
For all her love, she cannot tell
Whether I use it ill or well,
Nor knock at dusty doors to find
Her beauty dusty in the mind.

If the grave's gates could be undone,
She would not know her little son,
I am so grown. If we should meet,
She would pass by me in the street,
Unless my soul's face let her see
My sense of what she did for me.

What have I done to keep in mind
My debt to her and womankind?
What woman's happier life repays
Her for those months of wretched days?
For all my mouthless body leech'd
Ere Birth's releasing hell was reach'd?

What have I done, or tried, or said
In thanks to that dear woman dead?
Men triumph over women still,
Men trample women's rights at will,
And man's lust roves the world untamed.

* * *

O grave, keep shut lest I be shamed!

The Girl on the Land

'When have I known a boy
Kinder than this my daughter, or his kiss
More filial, or the clasping of his joy
    Closer than this?'

Thus did a mother think;
And yet her daughter had been long away,
Estranged, on other business; but the link
    Was fast today.

This mother, who was she?
I know she was the earth, she was the land.
Her daughter, a gay girl, toiled happily,
    Sheaves in hand.

The Modern Mother

    Oh, what a kiss
With filial passion overcharged is this!
    To this misgiving breast
This child runs, as a child ne'er ran to rest
Upon the light heart and the unoppressed.

    Unhoped, unsought!
A little tenderness this mother thought
    The utmost of her meed.
She looked for gratitude; content indeed
With thus much that her nine years' love had bought.

    Nay, even with less.
This mother, giver of life, death, peace, distress,
    Desired, ah! not so much
Thanks as forgiveness; and the passing touch
Expected, and the slight, the brief caress.

    O filial light
Strong in these childish eyes, these new, these bright
    Intelligible stars! Their rays
Are near the constant earth, guides in the maze,
Natural, true, keen in this dusk of days.

To My Mother
Written in a Pocket-Book, 1822

They tell us of an Indian tree
  Which, howsoe'er the sun and sky
May tempt its boughs to wander free,
  And shoot and blossom, wide and high,
Far better loves to bend its arms
  Downward again to that dear earth
From which the life, that fills and warms
  Its grateful being, first had birth.

'Tis thus, though wooed by flattering friends,
  And fed with fame (*if* fame it be),
This heart, my own dear mother, bends,
  With love's true instinct, to thee.

Song

Oh, baby, baby, baby dear,
We lie alone together here;
The snowy gown and cap and sheet
With lavender are fresh and sweet;
Through half-closed blinds the roses peer
To see and love you, baby dear.

You are so tired, we like to lie
Just doing nothing, you and I,
Within the darkened quiet room.
The sun sends dusk rays through the gloom,
Which is no gloom since you are here,
My little life, my baby dear.

Soft sleepy mouth so vaguely pressed
Against your new-made mother's breast.
Soft little hands in mine I fold,
Soft little feet I kiss and hold,
Round soft smooth head and tiny ear,
All mine, my own, my baby dear.

And he we love is far away!
But he will come some happy day,
You need but me, and I can rest
At peace with you beside me pressed.
There are no questions, longings vain,
No murmurings, no doubt, nor pain,
Only content and we are here,
            My baby dear.

'Granny Please Comb My Hair'

Granny Granny
please comb my hair
you always take your time
you always take such care

You put me to sit on a cushion
between your knees
you rub a little coconut oil
parting gentle as a breeze

Mummy Mummy
she's always in a hurry – hurry
rush
she pulls my hair
sometimes she tugs

But Granny
you have all the time in the world
and when you've finished
you always turn my head and say
'Now who's a nice girl.'

Written on Seeing Her Two Sons at Play

Sweet age of blest illusion! blooming boys,
Ah, revel long in childhood's thoughtless joys
With light and pliant spirits, that can stoop
To follow, sportively, the rolling hoop;
To watch the sleeping top with gay delight,
Or mark, with raptured gaze, the sailing kite;
Or, eagerly pursuing Pleasure's call,
Can find it centred on the bounding ball!
Alas! the day will come when sports like these
Must lose their magic and their power to please:
Too swiftly fled, the rosy hours of youth
Shall yield their fairy charms to mournful truth.
Even now a mother's fond prophetic fear
Sees the dark train of human ills appear;
Views various fortune for each lovely child,
Storms for the bold, and anguish for the mild;
Beholds already those expressive eyes
Beam a sad certainty of future sighs;
And dreads each suffering those dear breasts may know
In their long passage through a world of woe,
Perchance predestined every pang to prove,
That treacherous friends inflict, or faithless love.
For, ah! how few have found existence sweet,
Where grief is sure, but happiness deceit!

The Toys

My little Son, who look'd from thoughtful eyes
And moved and spoke in quiet grown-up wise,
Having my law the seventh time disobey'd,
I struck him, and dismiss'd
With hard words and unkiss'd,
His Mother, who was patient, being dead.
Then, fearing lest his grief should hinder sleep,
I visited his bed,
But found him slumbering deep,
With darken'd eyelids, and their lashes yet
From his late sobbing wet.
And I, with moan,
Kissing away his tears, left others of my own;
For, on a table drawn beside his head,
He had put, within his reach,
A box of counters and a red-vein'd stone,
A piece of glass abraded by the beach
And six or seven shells,
A bottle with bluebells,
And two French copper coins, ranged here with careful art,
To comfort his sad heart.
So when that night I pray'd
To God, I wept, and said:
Ah, when at last we lie with tranced breath,
Not vexing Thee in death,
And Thou rememberest of what toys
We made our joys,
How weakly understood,
Thy great commanded good,
Then, fatherly not less
Than I whom Thou hast moulded from the clay,

Thou'lt leave Thy wrath, and say,
'I will be sorry for their childishness.'

Squeezes

We love to squeeze bananas,
We love to squeeze ripe plums,
And when they are feeling sad
We love to squeeze our mums.

To Miss Charlotte Pulteney in Her Mother's Arms, 1 May 1724

Timely blossom, infant fair,
Fondling of a happy pair,
Every morn, and every night,
Their solicitous delight,
Sleeping, waking, still at ease,
Pleasing, without skill to please,
Little gossip, blithe and hale,
Tattling many a broken tale,
Singing many a tuneless song,
Lavish of a heedless tongue,
Simple maiden, void of art,
Babbling out the very heart,
Yet abandoned to thy will,
Yet imagining no ill,
Yet too innocent to blush,
Like the linlet in the bush,
To the mother-linnet's note
Moduling her slender throat,
Chirping forth thy petty joys,
Wanton in the change of toys,
Like the linnet green, in May,
Flitting to each bloomy spray,
Wearied then, and glad of rest,
Like the linlet in the nest.
This thy present happy lot,
This, in time, will be forgot:

Other pleasures, other cares,
Ever-busy time prepares;
And thou shalt in thy daughter see,
This picture, once, resembled thee.

Mater Desiderata

I cannot guess her face or form;
　But what to me is form or face?
I do not ask the weary worm
　To give me back each buried grace
Of glistening eyes or trailing tresses.
　I only feel that she is here,
　　　And that we meet, and that we part;
　And that I drink within mine ear,
　　　And that I clasp around my heart
Her sweet still voice and soft caresses.

Not in the waking thought by day,
　Nor in the sightless dream by night,
Do the mild tones and glances play
　Of her who was my cradle's light!
But in some twilight of calm weather
　She glides by fancy dimly wrought,
　　　A glittering cloud, a darkling beam,
　With all the quiet of a thought
　　　And all the passion of a dream
Link'd in a golden spell together.

On the Infancy of Our Saviour

Hail, blessed Virgin, full of heavenly grace,
Blest above all that sprang from human race;
Whose heaven-saluted womb brought forth in one
A blessed Saviour and a blessed Son.
Oh, what a ravishment it had been to see
Thy little Saviour perking on thy knee!
To see Him nuzzle in thy virgin-breast,
His milk-white body all unclad, undressed!
To see thy busy fingers clothe and wrap
His spreading limbs in thy indulgent lap!
To see His desperate eyes with childish grace
Smiling upon His smiling mother's face!
And when his forward strength began to bloom,
To see Him diddle up and down the room!
Oh, who would think so sweet a Babe as this
Should e'er be slain by a false-hearted kiss!
Had I a rag, if, sure, Thy body wore it,
Pardon, sweet Babe, I think I should adore it!
Till then, O grant this boon (a boon, or dearer),
The weed not being, I may adore the wearer.

In Praise of Women in General

He is a parricide to his mother's name,
And with an impious hand murders her fame,
That wrongs the praise of women: that dares write
Libels on saints, or with foul ink requite
The milk they lent us. Better sex, command
To your defence my more religious hand
At sword, or pen: yours was the nobler birth,
For you of man were made, man but of earth,
The son of dust; and though your sin did breed
His fall, again you raised him in your seed:
Adam in his sleep a gainful loss sustained,
That for one rib a better self regained;
Who, had he not your blest creation seen,
An anchorite in paradise had been.
Why in this work did the creation rest,
But that eternal providence thought you best
Of all his six days' labour? Beasts should do
Homage to man, but man should wait on you.
You are of comelier sight, of daintier touch,
A tender flesh, a colour bright, and such
As Parians see in marble; skin more fair,
More glorious head, and far more glorious hair,
Eyes full of grace and quickness; purer roses
Blush in your cheeks; a milder white composes
Your stately fronts; your breath more sweet than his
Breathes spice, and nectar drops at every kiss.
Your skins are smooth, bristles on theirs do grow
Like quills of porcupines; rough wool doth flow
O'er all their faces, you approach more near

The form of angels; they like beasts appear.
If then in bodies where the souls do dwell
You better us, do then our souls excel?
No; we in souls equal perfection see:
There can in them nor male nor female be.
Boast we of knowledge? You have more than we:
You were the first ventured to pluck the tree.
And, that more rhetoric in your tongues doth lie,
Let him dispute against that dares deny
Your least commands, and not persuaded be
With Samson's strength and David's piety
To be your willing captives. Virtue sure
Were blind as Fortune, should she choose the poor
Rough cottage man to live in, and despise
To dwell in you, the stately edifice.
Thus you are proved the better sex, and we
Must all repent that in our pedigree
We choose the father's name, where, should we take
The mother's (a more honoured blood), 'twould make
Our generation sure and certain be,
And I'd believe some faith in heraldry!
Thus, perfect creatures, if detraction rise
Against your sex, dispute but with your eyes,
Your hand, your lip, your brow: there will be sent
So subtle and so strong an argument,
Will teach the Stoic his affection too,
And call the Cynic from his tub to woo.
Thus mustering up your beauteous troops, go on:
The fairest is the valiant Amazon.

Purple Shoes

Mum and me had a row yesterday,
a big, exploding
howdareyouspeaktomelikethatI'mofftostayatGran's
kind of row.

It was about shoes.
I'd seen a pair of purple ones at Carter's,
heels not too high, soft suede, silver buckles;
'No,' she said.
'Not suitable for school.
I can't afford to buy rubbish.'
That's when we had our row.
I went to bed longing for those shoes.
They made footsteps in my mind,
kicking up dance dust;
I wore them in my dreams across a shiny floor,
under flashing coloured lights.
It was ruining my life not to have them.

This morning they were mine.
Mum relented and gave me the money.
I walked out of the store wearing new purple shoes.
I kept seeing myself reflected in shop windows
with purple shoes on,
walking to the bus stop,
walking the whole length of our street
wearing purple shoes.

On Monday I shall go to school in purple shoes.
Mum will say no a thousand furious times
But I don't care.
I'm not going to give in.

Ettykett

My mother knew a lot about manners,
   she said you should never slurp;
you should hold your saucer firmly,
   and not clang your teeth on the curp.

My father knew nothing of manners,
   all he could do was slurp;
and when I can't find a rhyming word,
   I set about making them urp.

For a Child Expected

Lovers whose lifted hands are candles in winter,
Whose gentle ways like streams in the easy summer,
Lying together
For secret setting of a child, love what they do,
Thinking they make that candle immortal, those streams
   forever flow,
And yet do better than they know.

So the first flutter of a baby felt in the womb,
Its little signal and promise of riches to come,
Is taken in its father's name;
Its life is the body of his love, like his caress,
First delicate and strange, that daily use
Makes dearer and priceless.

Our baby was to be the living sign of our joy,
Restore to each the other's lost infancy;
To a painter's pillaging eye
Poet's coiled hearing, add the heart we might earn
By the help of love; all that our passion would yield
We put to planning our child.

The world flowed in; whatever we liked we took:
For its hair, the gold curls of the November oak
We saw on our walk;
Snowberries that make a Milky Way in the wood
For its tender hands; calm screen of the frozen flood
For our care of its childhood.

But the birth of a child is an uncontrollable glory;
Cat's cradle of hopes will hold no living baby,

Long though it lay quietly.
And when our baby stirs and struggles to be born
It compels humility: what we began
Is now its own.

For *as the sun that shines through glass*
So Jesus in His Mother was.
Therefore every human creature,
Since it shares in His nature,
In candle-gold passion or white
Sharp star should show its own way of light.
May no paternal dread or dream
Darken our darling's early beam:
May she grow to her right powers
Unperturbed by passion of ours.

Dressed to Spill

A few tips for the first-time mum,
There's great joy, heaven knows,
But some adjustments must be made
When it comes to clothes.

Though once you were quite elegant,
Dressed with care and style,
Believe me, standards start to plunge
And stay there for some while.

It's goodbye to those power suits,
It's breast not shoulder pad,
And your vital accessory?
A well-stocked changing bag!

It's also time to say goodbye
To linen and to silk.
Hello to fabrics that hold their own
With regurgitated milk.

How to protect one's clothing,
Is something of a riddle;
No matter what, you'll be adorned
By Babe's own-label dribble.

Whenever Baby does a burp
One fact you'll have to face,
No matter where that muslin is
IT WON'T BE THE RIGHT PLACE.

So please do take this sound advice
And try to fill that closet
Exclusively with garments
That tone just right with posset!

'Mummy Said The "B" Word'

'Oooh, Mum,
You said the "B" word!
I heard you, Mum, just now.
You called the lady in that car
A bloody selfish cow!'

'It's okay, Mum,
Don't worry.
I promise – won't tell Dad.
We all know swearing's wicked
And the "B" word's very bad!'

'Hey, Dad,
Mum said the "B" word,
A lady took her space,
She said it very loudly
Went bright red in the face.
And then she told the husband
He had a bloody nerve.
You see, she said it twice, Dad –
And what's an effing perve?'

'Meekly We Sing and Say to Thee'

Meekly we sing and say to thee,
'*Maria, spes nostra, salue.*'

Children of Eve, both great and small,
  Here in this vale of wretchedness
With great weeping to thee we call
  For help and grace in our distress,
  And, as our tongues can express,
    Meekly we sing to thee,
    '*Maria, spes nostra, salue.*'

Thou art, lady, and ever shalt be,
  Queen of mercy, mother of grace;
Therefore at need, O lady free,
  Turn unto us thy glorious face
  And comfort us in every case,
    Since we do sing and say to thee,
    '*Maria, spes nostra, salue.*'

Though it be much that we offend,
  Yet we be thine for evermore;
Therefore thy grace to us extend,
  Pure virgin, after and before;
  For sin that we be not forlore,
    Since we do sing and say to thee,
    '*Maria, spes nostra, salue.*'

Thou dost abound so in all ways
  With goodness, grace, and all virtue,
So that our laud cannot suffice
  To thee, sweet mother of Jesu;

But yet our prayers not eschew,
    Since we do sing and say to thee,
    'Maria, spes nostra, salue.'

Sweet and benign mediatrix,
  Thine eyen of grace on us thou cast,
Since thou art queen of paradise,
  And let not our hope be in waste,
  But show us thy Son at the last,
    Since we do sing and say to thee,
    'Maria, spes nostra, salue.'

O meek and mild, full of pity,
  For us pray to that Prince of Peace
That we may come to that city
  Whereof the joy shall never cease
  But multiply and ever increase,
    Since we do sing and say to thee,
    'Maria, spes nostra, salue.'

'Mother Wept, and Father Sigh'd'

Mother wept, and father sigh'd;
　　With delight aglow
Cried the lad, 'Tomorrow,' cried,
　　'To the pit I go.'

Up and down the place he sped, –
　　Greeted old and young;
Far and wide the tidings spread;
　　Clapt his hands and sung.

Came his cronies; some to gaze
　　Wrapp'd in wonder; some
Free with counsel; some with praise;
　　Some with envy dumb.

'May he,' many a gossip cried,
　　'Be from peril kept.'
Father hid his face and sigh'd,
　　Mother turn'd and wept.

from *The Dream*

Thus leaving them I passed on my way;
But ere that I had little further gone,
I saw a fierce insatiable foe,
Depopulating countries, sparing none:
Without respect of age, sex, or degree,
It did devour, and could not daunted be.

Some feared this foe, some loved it as a friend;
For though none could the force of it withstand,
Yet some by it were sent to Tophet's flames,
But others led to heavenly Canaan land:
On some it seized with a gentle power,
And others furiously it did devour.

The name of this impartial foe was Death,
Whose rigour, whilst I furiously did view,
Upon a sudden, ere I was aware,
With piercing dart my mother dear it slew,
Which, when I saw, it made me so to weep
That tears and sobs did rouse me from my sleep.

But, when I waked, I found my dream was true;
For Death had ta'en my mother's breath away,
Though of her life it could not her bereave,
Since she in glory lives with Christ for aye;
Which makes me glad, and thankful for her bliss,
Though still bewail her absence whom I miss.

A sudden sorrow pierceth to the quick;
Speedy encounters fortitude doth try;
Unarmed men receive the deepest wound,
Expected perils time doth lenify;
Her sudden loss hath cut my feeble heart
So deep that daily I endure the smart.

To Alison Cunningham From Her Boy

For the long nights you lay awake
And watched for my unworthy sake:
For your most comfortable hand
That led me through the uneven land:
For all the story-books you read:
For all the pains you comforted:
For all you pitied, all you bore,
In sad and happy days of yore: –
My second mother, my first wife,
The angel of my infant life –
From the sick child, now well and old,
Take, nurse, the little book you hold!

And grant it, heaven, that all who read
May find as dear a nurse at need,
And every child who lists my rhyme,
In the bright, fireside, nursery clime,
May hear it in as kind a voice
As made my childish days rejoice!

To My Mother

You too, my mother, read my rhymes
For love of unforgotten times,
And you may chance to hear once more
The little feet along the floor.

To Any Reader

As from the house your mother sees
You playing round the garden trees,
So you may see, if you will look
Through the windows of this book,
Another child, far, far away,
And in another garden, play.
But do not think you can at all,
By knocking on the window, call
That child to hear you. He intent
Is all on his play-business bent.
He does not hear; he will not look,
Nor yet be lured out of this book.
For, long ago, the truth to say,
He has grown up and gone away,
And it is but a child of air
That lingers in the garden there.

A Mother's Love

There's beauty in the breath of morn,
  When earth is bright with dew and light,
When summer buds and flowers are born –
  And clouds seem angels on their flight!
There's joy which innocence imparts,
  A sweetness every breast may prove;
But what's so sweet to human hearts,
  So precious, as a mother's love?

The sun to light the east may fail,
  The morn forsake her fields of dew,
The silvery clouds forget to sail
  Along their sea of heavenly blue;
And all that's bright may pass away –
  Our hopes recall, our friends remove,
Yet, constant, 'midst a world's decay,
  Still sweet would be a mother's love.

from *Demeter and Persephone (In Enna)*

So in this pleasant vale we stand again,
The field of Enna, now once more ablaze
With flowers that brighten as thy footstep falls,
All flowers – but for one black blur of earth
Left by that closing chasm, through which the car
Of dark Aidoneus rising rapt thee hence.
And here, my child, though folded in thine arms,
I feel the deathless heart of motherhood
Within me shudder, lest the naked glebe
Should yawn once more into the gulf, and thence
The shrilly whinnyings of the team of Hell,
Ascending, pierce the glad and songful air,
And all at once their arched necks, midnight-maned,
Jet upward through the mid-day blossom. No!
For, see, thy foot has touched it; all the space
Of blank earth-baldness clothes itself afresh,
And breaks into the crocus-purple hour
That saw thee vanish.

              Child, when thou wert gone,
I envied human wives, and nested birds,
Yea, the cubbed lioness; went in search of thee
Through many a palace, many a cot, and gave
Thy breast to ailing infants in the night,
And set the mother waking in amaze
To find her sick one whole; and forth again
Among the wail of midnight winds, and cried,
'Where is my loved one? Wherefore do ye wail?'
And out from all the night an answer shrilled,
'We know not, and we know not why we wail.'

I climbed on all the cliffs of all the seas,
And asked the waves that moan about the world
'Where? do ye make your moanings for my child?'
And round from all the world the voices came
'We know not, and we know not why we moan.'
'Where?' and I stared from every eagle-peak,
I thridded the black heart of all the woods,
I peered through tomb and cave, and in the storms
Of Autumn swept across the city, and heard
The murmur of their temples chanting me,
Me, me, the desolate Mother! 'Where?' – and turned,
And fled by many a waste, forlorn of man,
And grieved for man through all my grief for thee, –
The jungle rooted in his shattered hearth,
The serpent coiled about his broken shaft,
The scorpion crawling over naked skulls; –
I saw the tiger in the ruined fane
Spring from his fallen god, but trace of thee
I saw not; and far on, and, following out
A league of labyrinthine darkness, came
On three grey heads beneath a gleaming rift.
'Where?' and I heard one voice from all the three
'We know not, for we spin the lives of men,
And not of gods, and know not why we spin!
There is a fate beyond us.' Nothing knew . . .

'Little Jesus'

Little Jesus, wast Thou shy
Once, and just as small as I?
And what did it feel like to be
Out of heaven, and just like me?
Didst Thou sometimes think of *there*,
And ask where all the angels were?
I should think that I would cry
For my house all made of sky;
I would look about the air,
And wonder where my angels were;
And at waking 'twould distress me –
Not an angel there to dress me!
Hadst Thou ever any toys,
Like us little girls and boys?
And didst Thou play in heaven with all
The angels that were not too tall,
With stars for marbles? Did the things
Play *Can you see me?* through their wings?
And did Thy mother let Thee spoil
Thy robes, with playing on *our* soil?
How nice to have them always new
In heaven, because 'twas quite clean blue!

Didst Thou kneel at night to pray,
And didst Thou join Thy hands, this way?
And did they tire sometimes, being young,
And make the prayers seem very long?
And dost Thou like it best, that we
Should join our hands to pray to Thee?
I used to think, before I knew,

The prayer not said unless we do.
And did Thy mother at the night
Kiss Thee, and fold the clothes in right?
And didst Thou feel quite good in bed,
Kiss'd, and sweet, and Thy prayers said?

Thou canst not have forgotten all
That it feels like to be small:
And Thou know'st I cannot pray
To Thee in my father's way –
When Thou wast so little, say,
Couldst Thou talk Thy Father's way? –

So, a little Child, come down
And hear a child's tongue like Thy own;
Take me by the hand and walk,
And listen to my baby-talk.
To Thy Father show my prayer
(He will look, Thou art so fair),
And say: 'O Father, I, Thy Son,
Bring the prayer of a little one.'

And He will smile, that children's tongue
Has not changed since Thou wast young!

Sonnet Addressed to My Mother

O thou, whose tender smile most partially
  Hath ever blessed thy child – to thee belong
  The graces which adorn my first wild song,
If aught of grace it knows, nor thou deny
Thine ever-prompt attention to supply.
  But let me lead thy willing ear along
  Where virtuous love still bids the strain prolong
His innocent applause since, from thine eye,
  The beams of love first charmed my infant breast,
And from thy lip Attention's soothing voice
  That eloquence of tenderness expressed,
Which still my grateful heart confessed divine –
Oh ever may its accents sweet rejoice
The soul which loves to own whate'er it has is thine!

The Sailor's Mother

One morning (raw it was, and wet –
A foggy day in winter time)
A woman on the road I met,
Not old, though something past her prime:
Majestic in her person, tall and straight;
And like a Roman matron's was her mien and gait.

The ancient spirit is not dead;
Old times, thought I, are breathing there;
Proud was I that my country bred
Such strength, a dignity so fair.
She begged an alms, like one in poor estate;
I looked at her again, nor did my pride abate.

When from these lofty thoughts I woke,
'What is it,' said I, 'that you bear
Beneath the covert of your cloak,
Protected from this cold, damp air?'
She answered, soon as she the question heard,
'A simple burden, sir, a little singing-bird'.

And, thus continuing, she said:
'I had a son who, many a day
Sailed on the seas, but he is dead:
In Denmark he was cast away,
And I have travelled weary miles to see
If aught which he had owned might still remain for me.

'The bird and cage they both were his:
'Twas my son's bird; and neat and trim
He kept it: many voyages
The singing-bird had gone with him;
When last he sailed he left the bird behind,
From bodings, as might be, that hung upon his mind.

'He to a fellow lodger's care
Had left it, to be watched and fed,
And pipe its song in safety; – there
I found it when my son was dead;
And now, God help me for my little wit,
I bear it with me, sir – he took so much delight in it'.

The Cottager to Her Infant

The days are cold, the nights are long,
The north-wind sings a doleful song;
Then hush again upon my breast;
All merry things are now at rest,
      Save thee, my pretty love!

The kitten sleeps upon the hearth,
The crickets long have ceased their mirth;
There's nothing stirring in the house
Save one wee, hungry, nibbling mouse,
      Then why so busy thou?

Nay, start not at that sparkling light;
'Tis but the moon that shines so bright
On the window pane bedropped with rain:
Then, little darling, sleep again,
      And wake when it is day.

Confirmation Continued

I saw a mother's eye intensely bent
Upon a maiden trembling as she knelt,
In and for whom the pious mother felt
Things that we judge of by a light too faint:
Tell, if ye may, some star-crowned muse or saint,
Tell what rushed in, from what she was relieved,
Then, when her child the hallowing touch received,
And such vibration through the mother went
That tears burst forth amain. Did gleams appear?
Opened a vision of that blissful place
Where dwells a sister-child? And was power given
Part of her lost one's glory back to trace
Even to this rite? For thus she knelt, and, ere
The summer leaf had faded, passed to heaven.

To Mira, On the Care of Her Infant

Mira, as thy dear Edward's senses grow,
Be sure they all will seek this point – *to know*.
Woo to enquiry – strictures long avoid;
By force the thirst of weakly sense is cloyed:
Silent attend the frown, the gaze, the smile,
To grasp far objects the incessant toil;
So play life's springs with energy, and try
The unceasing thirst of knowledge to supply.

   I saw the beauteous Caleb t' other day
Stretch forth his little hand to touch a spray,
Whilst on the grass his drowsy nurse inhaled
The sweets of nature as her sweets exhaled.
But, ere the infant reached the playful leaf,
She pulled him back – his eyes o'erflowed with grief;
He checked his tears – her fiercer passions strove,
She looked a vulture cowering o'er a dove!
'I'll teach you, brat!' The pretty trembler sighed –
When, with a cruel shake, she hoarsely cried –
'Your mother spoils you – everything you see
You covet. It shall ne'er be so with me!
Here, eat this cake, sit still, and don't you rise –
Why don't you pluck the sun down from the skies?
I'll spoil your sport – Come, laugh me in the face –
And henceforth learn to keep your proper place.
You rule me in the house! To hush your noise
I, like a spaniel, must run for toys:
But here, sir, let the trees alone, nor cry –
Pluck if you dare – Who's master, you or I?'

   Oh brutal force, to check the enquiring mind
When it would pleasure in a rosebud find!

~ List of Latin Translations

Anon, fifteenth century, 'Noel, el, el, el, el, el, el…', l. 6 *Gabriel nuntio*: Gabriel being the messenger; l.10 *Cum… lilio*: by the lily of modesty (the lily is an emblem of Mary's virginity); l.14 *Fulget resurrectio*: [His] resurrection blazes forth; l. 18 *Motu…proprio*: borne by His own desire (or impulse); l. 22 *In…palatio*: in the heavenly temple.

John Audelay, 'The Mother of Mary', l. 43 *Mater…Filium*: Mother, pray to your Son; ll. 45-6 *Nobis…fine*: give us joy without end.

Richard Edwards, '*Amantium Irae Amoris Redintegratio*': the title is translated as the refrain.

Emilia Lanier, [*A Defence of Eve*]: the title of the work from which the extract is taken, *Salve Deus Rex Judaeorum*, means 'Hail, God, King of the Jews'.

Winthrop Mackworth Praed, '*Mater Desiderata*': the title means 'the longed-for mother'.

James Ryman, '*Meekly We Sing and Say to Thee*', l. 2 *Maria…salue*: Mary, our hope, greetings.

~ *Index of Titles or First Lines*

~ *Acknowledgements*

The editor and publishers wish to thank the following for permission to use copyright or archive material:

Anon, 'Noel, el, el, el, el, el, el,...', MS Sloane 2593, by agreement of The British Library; John Agard, 'Ask Mummy Ask Daddy' from *I Din Do Nuttin* by John Agard, Bodley Head, by permission of The Random House Group Ltd; Allan Ahlberg, 'Emma Hackett's Newsbook' and 'Our Mother' from *Please Mrs Butler* by Allan Ahlberg, Kestrel (1983). Copyright © Allan Ahlberg, 1983, by permission of Penguin Books Ltd; John Audelay, 'The Mother of Mary', MS Douce 302, fol. 31r-v, by agreement with The Bodleian Library, University of Oxford; Sir John Betjeman, extract 'Percival Mandeville, the Perfect Boy' from *Summoned by Bells* by John Betjeman and 'False Security' from *Collected Poems* by John Betjeman, by permission of John Murray (Publishers) Ltd; Elizabeth Brewster, 'Magnolia Avenue' from *Selected Poems* by Elizabeth Brewster, by permission of Oberon Press; Charles Causley, 'My Mother Saw a Dancing Bear' and 'What Has Happened to Lulu?' from *Figgie Hoban* by Charles Causley, Macmillan (1970), by permission of David Higham Associates on behalf of the author; Roald Dahl, 'The Price of Debauchery' and 'Mary, Mary' from *Rhyme Stew* by Roald Dahl, Jonathan Cape and Penguin Books, by permission of David Higham Associates on behalf of the Estate of the author; Trevor Harvey, 'The Painting Lesson', first published in *Funny Poems*, ed. Heather Amery, Usborne (1990), by permission of the author; Mary Ann Hoberman, 'Brother' from *The Llama Who Had No Pajama* by Mary Ann Hoberman. Copyright © 1959, renewed 1987, 1998 by Mary Ann Hoberman, by permission of Gina Maccoby Literary Agency on